How Old Is Your Soul?

The Essential Guide to the Lessons, Gifts and Archetypes of Every Soul Age

BY ALYSSA MALEHORN

RAW SPIRITUALITY
AUSTIN, TX
USA

HOW OLD IS YOUR SOUL?
THE ESSENTIAL GUIDE TO THE LESSONS, GIFTS AND ARCHETYPES OF EVERY SOUL AGE

Front cover design by Zack Fuentes
Cover image by Daniel Holeman
Editing and design by Sara Zibrat

ISBN 978-0-9979914-0-6
Library of Congress Control Number: 2016914169

Publisher's Cataloging-In-Publication Data
(Prepared by The Donohue Group, Inc.)

Names: Malehorn, Alyssa.
Title: How old is your soul? : the essential guide to the lessons, gifts and archetypes of every soul age / by Alyssa Malehorn.
Description: Austin, TX, USA : Raw Spirituality, [2016]
Identifiers: LCCN 2016914169 | ISBN 978-0-9979914-0-6 | ISBN 978-0-9979914-1-3 (ebook)
Subjects: LCSH: Soul. | Spiritual life. | Conduct of life. | Chakras.
Classification: LCC BL290 .M35 2016 (print) | LCC BL290 (ebook) | DDC 202.2--dc23

Published by:
Raw Spirituality
Austin, Texas 78746
USA

This paper meets the requirements of ANSI/NISO 239.48-1992 (Permanence of Paper).

DEDICATION

For Zack, my spiritual partner in all things:

Thank you for finding me like you promised, knocking
on my door and bringing the real love with you. As we
support and guide each other through the maya, with eyes
on the Light within and around, acknowledging the I AM
in ourselves, each other, and all living things,
we still have much to spirit-adventure together!

You are Light.

~ ~ ~

For my greatest joy, Wolfgang:

Thank you for choosing me as your earthly mother,
teaching me a new way to love,
and with a depth I couldn't have dreamt,
and for sharing your infinite journey with me.

You are Love.

~ ~ ~

For my parents, Sue and Gary:
I honor you and am supremely blessed to be your
daughter.

Thank you for taking on the mission, with your brave,
unwavering hearts! Words cannot express the depth of
love, respect and gratitude.

You are Peace.

~ ~ ~

For my sister and soul sisters, Angela, Renee, Krista, Pam, Lauren, Charlotte, Betty, Karen, Danielle, Shannon, Lacey, Maureen and the rest of you beautiful, boundless beings, both incarnate and on the other side, you know who you are: I am humbled and uplifted by your love, grateful for you every day, and empowered by your side, as we share this adventure.

You are Infinite.

~ ~ ~

For my students, clients, colleagues and readers: You inspire my continued growth and breathe life into my work. Thank you.

You are Inspiration.

~ ~ ~

For the Great Spirit, Council of Light, Highest and Purest Guides, Angels and Archangels, and Ascended Masters: Thank you, thank you, thank you.

I AM.

TABLE OF CONTENTS

INTRODUCTION

HAVE YOU EVER FELT LIKE YOU WERE AN OLDER SOUL? Or that everyone around you was different than you, and that you didn't fit into today's world? It's not unusual for mature and older souls to feel like a fish out of water. When I use the terms "Mature" or "Old Soul," I'm referring to souls who have incarnated many, many times, and are well on their way to enlightenment.

This doesn't mean that the older your soul is, the easier your life will be. It can be far different than expectations of choirs of angels and peaceful feelings all the time! It only means that those of us who are in the Mature and Old Soul levels typically see the world in much the same way, and we all go through a similar process of healing.

This information in this book arose from the experiences I've had in years of working with and helping clients and students who, as a group, are almost entirely older souls. I relate to the depth of feelings of my dear clients and students, as I am an older soul as well. We all share so many traits, challenges, and milestones. You wouldn't be attracted to this writing if you weren't also in that older soul phase. *How Old Is Your Soul?* came into being to help make your road a little less rocky, with more light to guide the way.

The intention of this book is to help you to see the motivations, gifts and struggles inherent within each soul age, so that you can live without judgment of others and without judgment of yourself. I believe that understanding these concepts is the key to relaxing into life, releasing expectations of yourself and others that aren't based in the soul's true nature.

It's common for mature and old souls to feel things so deeply that depression or anxiety can become a pattern, get locked in, and become the new normal. The following pages not only contain information about who you are in your own soul phase and what to do about it, but the words on these pages are also transmitting healing, transformational energy to you, and if you're highly sensitive, you'll even feel it.

Part 1 of This Book covers the mind, body, soul and spirit complex, how our individual souls develop and grow, karma, and much more about our human process in general. Part 2 covers each of the soul ages, so you can understand other people in your life and the path your soul has taken up to this point. To fully absorb the healing that's available for you here, I encourage you to take the time to do the exercises and meditations at the end of each chapter. These tools are designed to help you more fully understand your spiritual journey, transcend fear, resolve the past, and elevate into inner peace and harmony.

I'm very grateful to be your guide on this journey, and I'm honored to work with you in this way. I have so much love for you. Thank you.

Blessings to you,
Alyssa

~ PART 1 ~

THE FRAMEWORK OF SOUL EXPANSION

"The soul's natural state is freedom."

~ CHAPTER 1 ~

THE SOUL & HOW IT GROWS

"Only as a warrior can one withstand the path of knowledge. A warrior cannot complain or regret anything. His life is an endless challenge, and challenges cannot possibly be good or bad. Challenges are simply challenges." ~ Carlos Castaneda

WE ARE ALL MULTIDIMENSIONAL BEINGS, with a mind, a body, a soul, and a spirit. That four-part complex of energy holds every aspect of us within it. Each of these components of our complete being is equally important, although each has its natural state and its natural gifts. When we fully understand these aspects of ourselves and the role that each part plays, we begin to live more authentic lives. We edge closer and closer to our true nature, and life changes dramatically for the positive. These aspects (the mind, body, soul and spirit) overlap and operate synergistically in a dynamic, awe-inspiring way.

In popular culture in recent years, there has been a growing focus on spirituality. This is because everyone on the planet is evolving spiritually, and looking for guidance and answers as they shift out of spiritual slumber into an awakened state of deeper authenticity. All humans are craving healing on a soul level, wanting to feel happy and complete. The soul's growth is the key to achieving those goals. When you support yourself on a soul level, the rest of you—your mind, body and spirit—all fall into alignment, and voila! You're happy! This is the reason for this book: to facilitate your soul's growth by guiding you along your spiritual path.

To begin that soul-supportive journey, we need to have some clarity about the entire four-part system, starting with your spirit. Your spirit is the part of you that knows your perfection and has no fear, the part of you that's always aware of and connected to your Divine Source. Can you imagine always having zero fear of anything and always knowing that you are an aspect of your Source? Your spirit holds that knowledge consistently and continuously, without any hesitation or doubt. On a spirit level, every one of us has a knowing that there is this part of us that can't ever be destroyed, manipulated or separated from Source. Somewhere deep within you, your spirit knows that you're just fine exactly the way you are, no matter what!

The spirit is beautiful and divine in every one of us, even in those who suffer with deep personal issues or who have committed horrible crimes. It can be hard to imagine that someone who's intentionally harmed another could have a pristine spirit, but they do. The spirit doesn't suffer, ever. It doesn't know darkness or fear, because it hasn't forgotten what you are. Your spirit knows that your true nature is eternal Source energy. Your true nature is light.

You know that glorious feeling that spontaneously happens when you're so full of gratitude or love for someone or something that it feels like your heart could just burst out of your chest? That's the way your spirit feels all of the time. When you get that incredible love-and-gratitude feeling, you're connecting into your magnificent spirit, your highest self.

There are many ways to access your spirit intentionally. My favorite ways are deep meditation and mindfulness/thankfulness practices, such as repeating a gratitude-based phrase (for example, "I am so blessed" or "I am thankful") many times until you feel your mood lift and your frequency rises to that awesome spirit-connected feeling.

Although it may seem unusual to be connected with that spirit part of you, it's actually totally normal and natural, and you arrived in this lifetime with that connection fully established, even if you haven't been aware of it before now. By picking up this book, you're already on your way to remembering your true nature.

Moving on to the second aspect of your four-part complex: your body. You'd think "the body" would be pretty self-explanatory, and in some ways it is, but I'd like to give you more of the big picture. Your body is your vehicle. Yes, your body is your physical self, made up of cells, tissue, organs, muscles, bones and DNA. But your body also includes something called the subtle body. The subtle body includes the energy field surrounding your body, what we call the aura. Together, your physical body and the subtle body make up your complete body.

The subtle body also includes the chakras or energy centers, along with the other layers and intricacies of your energy system. To dive into that deep pool of information about the subtle body wouldn't be appropriate for what we're exploring here, but just know that when your physical body dies, you have an energy body that continues to thrive. That energy body connects and blends with every other aspect of your beautiful being while you're here in physical form. When you're no longer in physical form and the physical body dies, the soul and the energy body are what live on.

Now, on to the third aspect of your four-part complex: your mind. This is the aspect of us that sometimes feels inferior, sometimes superior, sometimes lost, opinionated, fearful or loving, but it is not usually any one of those consistently. Our minds tend to sway with the turning of events in our lives, unable to stay centered or focused without some practice and work to deliberately train the mind to behave. Meditation is a good example of that type of work.

Our mind can be incredibly powerful. It can be used to support us in so many ways; help us move forward in every area of our lives; and to learn, retain and apply knowledge. But the mind also has a rebellious and fearful side. Because of that fear, it can contribute to our resisting our natural growth and spiritual evolution. Our mind tends to want to lead our entire life experience and, because of its fickle nature, it's certainly not qualified to do that. When we let our mind lead, all heck can break loose! It's not designed to be the head honcho of our human experience, and it doesn't have the wisdom and natural leadership ability of the soul. When we allow our mind to lead our life experience, the soul knows its power has been overthrown and it wants to be in its rightful role. The soul will ache to lead.

What does it feel like when your soul is aching to lead? The feelings of general overwhelm or dissatisfaction can be a subtle nagging in the back of your mind or an intense frustration, but either way, you know something is just "off" when your soul is unfulfilled. Most people on the planet right now have some degree of this as an ongoing issue. The mind or the body have been in the driver's seat for too long, and I'm going to help you correct that in the coming pages.

Speaking of the soul, let's get to it. Spiritually, this is the most important part of the four-part complex—the part of you that you're here to grow and develop. Your soul is the part of you—the true, authentic self—that has incarnated many times, some of us more than others. Your soul is who you really are. Every time you arrive here on Earth in a physical form, it's the result of a decision—a conscious choice made by you—to have a human lifetime in the specific family, geographic region, society, era and individual body that you've arrived in. Let that really sink in! You chose your parents, your eye color, where you were born, your intelligence level, and the challenges you were going to face in this lifetime. I must've thought I was a real badass before I was born, because I chose some interesting characteristics! (Picture the Southern Baptist deacon's daughter who was seeing dead people and talking to spirits in the hallway outside of Sunday School, for starters. Add serious "mystery illnesses" early in life and you've got the makings of a pretty tough chick.) With whatever you chose for yourself, I'm sure you must've thought you were pretty strong, too, and you'd be right. It takes a lot of courage to incarnate here. You have choices and you chose this life.

These multiple lifetimes are the most common method for our soul's evolution; your soul evolves, grows and develops in each and every lifetime. The soul drags your unresolved issues from one lifetime to the next, carrying that baggage in the mind and the body until it's healed. This can manifest in many different ways, as issues that show up early in life, such as illnesses, phobias, birth defects, learning challenges, abusive parents, and many other traits and situations that don't seem to make logical sense. We can heal those issues and the trauma that accompanies them, by discovering and connecting with the hidden treasure within each of us—our soul. As we resolve what we've carried with us from lifetime to lifetime, the process of healing those issues helps our soul to move along in its developmental journey.

In a nutshell, this explains why we would ever choose to experience challenging circumstances or traits in any lifetime. Why wouldn't we just choose to be born physically beautiful, with no health problems, no emotional issues, and to be born into a wealthy, loving family in a safe, nice neighborhood, without any problems at all? Because the more challenges we choose to overcome—the more we have to deal with—the more opportunities for our soul to grow. Believe it or not, your soul's growth was your top priority when you were making those pre-life choices. Your comfort and ideal life circumstances would only be chosen if those choices wouldn't interfere with your learning.

The most important thing to remember about your life is that *everything is an exercise*. Whatever the situation, it's an exercise. Everything that happens in your world—good things, painful things, everything—they are all exercises that we've chosen to experience for our soul's progress. No matter what it is, it's not personal. It's an exercise. You are always getting what you want on a soul level, in every circumstance, in every situation. It might not seem like what you want. You might say, "There's no way I wanted this! My job (spouse, friend, mom, dad, fill in the blank) is terrible! I want good things!" But your soul knows what it truly wants to experience, in order for you to eventually feel the freedom and love that's your Divine birthright.

Many people tend to feel victimized by life's painful events, illnesses, and betrayals, and are unwilling to believe that this life could be a soul-training and development experience, with this planet acting as our centralized training facility. We must consider accepting this as a higher truth as we step toward true, ever-growing happiness. This concept is very important for your success in the steps you're about to take. You don't have to believe it right this second, but for now, consider believing that it could potentially be true.

Interconnectedness and Remembering

Your spirit, mind, body and soul have an interesting relationship. In most of us, these four aspects are fragmented; they're not in alignment with each other at all. It's common for each aspect to be in competition with the others, attempting to lead your entire human experience and be the boss. It's even more common for us to rely solely on our mind when it's convenient, our body when it's convenient, our soul when it's convenient... you get the idea.

Why would you want to eliminate that competition between these aspects of self, and what are the side-effects of that lack of harmony? Self-judgment, self-criticism, overwhelm, physical and emotional exhaustion, repetition of painful experiences, and a feeling of disempowerment, for starters. There are more, but we'll get to that in the chapters on the specific soul ages. For now, know that there is relief coming.

Through integrating our four-part complex by using spiritual understanding and development, we can release the self-imposed barriers to that integration. These barriers are the beliefs, thoughts, ideas, feeling and patterns that we've accumulated throughout our lives. They contribute to an illusion of separation from our soul-selves and our Divine Source. Heal and release the barriers, and there we'll find our true essence. When we've done that, we've connected with the soul and we've reconnected our mind, body, soul and spirit all together as one. In the process, we begin to have a deep understanding and compassion for our own soul's path. This clarity then illuminates everyone else's soul path that we come across. Compassion and understanding gently overcome judgment and critical thoughts about ourselves and everyone else.

Sounds good, I know. Might sound impossible, but this is a natural, normal part of your development. You've just been in the dark, or without a map. Now we're starting to shed some light on the details of your soul, and this will all become more clear as we proceed.

To make things even more interesting, your body follows the cues from your mind. What your mind believes—consciously and unconsciously—gets imprinted on your body, your cells, your DNA. Your body is like a recorder that's just playing back what it's recorded from your mind (your thoughts, feelings, beliefs). What you think and what you believe in your mind, has convinced your body of its truth. Your mind is good at that, and your body is easily persuaded.

Your soul listens to your mind in a different way. Everything that your soul experiences, it sees as an opportunity to grow and learn. All of the bondage that your mind can project, such as thoughts that start with "I can't" or "I'm not good enough" or "If only" or "I'll be happy when... ," your soul doesn't believe it. Your soul's innate wisdom can see straight through that mind talk, regardless of the baggage and wounding you've brought along with you to resolve in this lifetime. How is it that your soul can see your limitless possibilities? It's simple. *The soul's natural state is freedom.*

Even though you've arrived in this world with some burdens and some gifts, in perfect proportion for your individual journey, and even though you may feel overwhelmed by said gifts and burdens at times, your soul has wisdom. It knows exactly what's going on with your body, your mind and, of course, your spirit. And the soul knows exactly how to work its way into that natural state of freedom, in the most efficient and effective way for you.

Everything that happens in your life—every feeling you have, every thought, fear, joy, anxiety, and challenge—is designed to help your soul develop, learn, evolve, and remember that you are a being of light. You incarnated for the "soul" purpose of remembering and re-awakening your natural light-self. Eventually, you'll have enough lifetimes to fully integrate your true divine self, your spirit. It's the nature of the soul to evolve this way, to consistently work toward remembering your light. And every experience that you have in this (and any other) lifetime is to support that work and to help you remember.

So yes, we're all in a growth process, a spiritual awakening, but more accurately, we're in a remembering process. This remembering of our own light is also called enlightenment, which I'm defining here as "perceiving reality accurately." When we're perceiving reality accurately, we've released all filters, such as the filter of victimization, where we perceive that everything is happening "to" us. Consider the filter of inferiority (where we never feel like we're up to par), the filter of superiority (where we're judging others), or the filter of unworthiness (where we are looking for evidence that we're unworthy). What about the filter of aging and what that says about our value as women or men or as human beings? When we're perceiving reality accurately—when we're enlightened—we experience life with no erroneous filters. Unconditional love and freedom are the foundations of our understanding. What an awesome thing—to know that we're not having to learn something that's completely foreign to us, or even a little bit unknown. We're just remembering. This is your natural state!

But from the first incarnation, from that very first moment when we chose to show up in physical form on the planet, we all have forgotten the natural state of freedom and the feeling of unconditional love from the

Divine, as well as the Divinity that resides within us. With every lifetime, we accumulate more remembering, more light. We remember more and more of who we really are, through experiences of all types with all sorts of outcomes. As we learn and grow in each lifetime, our priorities get more clear and we start to see that love is the only real priority; every time we're born, we temporarily forget, until we re-activate our spiritual journey, typically sometime in adulthood. At that predetermined point, we're able to integrate all of the learning from the previous lifetimes.

At that point, we may not have a conscious remembering in our minds of each incarnation or the lessons we learned. It's not typical to have a flood of past-life memories with giant "aha!" moments attached to them. In most people that's not the way it happens at all. Our soul helps us by allowing those lessons to appear in the mind and body when we're ready—neurologically, emotionally and physically. The evidence of that learning comes when our perceptions about ourselves and our lives shift, without an intentional, deliberate striving to achieve that shift. It's happening more and more these days. We're not done until we've worked our way back to our truth, completely and permanently. In a nutshell, that's the journey of our soul.

The Five Phase Blueprint

Fortunately, the soul's development comes with sort of a blueprint. There are five general levels or phases, and within each of those five levels there are several sub-levels. We each begin our journey as a newly created soul, straight from our Divine Source. In soul terms, we're like babies at that point. There aren't too many of these first-level "baby" souls on the planet at this time; they're pretty rare. As we are collectively wrapping up one Creation cycle (while another is dawning), there are no brand new souls being created, so as the infant souls are graduating up and out of this level, we have fewer and fewer of them.

After we've gotten a few lifetimes under our belts, we move into our second level, which resembles a young child stage. These souls are more plentiful right now than the new baby souls, but still are not in the majority. The progress continues into soul adolescence (the teenage years), level three. There are more level three souls on the planet right now than any other level.

Many lifetimes later, we enter the mature soul age, level four. Mature souls are less numerous than the level three adolescents, but more common than our next group, the elders or the old souls (level five). Remember there are many sub-levels within each level. Late-stage level five (old souls) have accumulated so much Divine light, wisdom and spiritual knowledge, you typically know them when you see them. If you're wondering where you fall into all of these levels of soul age, I've got a surprise for you. Most of you wouldn't be drawn to this book unless you were either a mature soul, an old soul or almost to that point. You may not always feel like you're just bursting with light or wisdom, but it's there in some form, for you to have gotten this far in your soul's development. In the chapters ahead, we'll go into detail about these levels and it will become more clear.

When we finish the complete soul cycle of development, we typically won't choose to incarnate anymore. We instead choose to help others who have incarnated by delivering guidance, inspiration and/or protection while we stay in the spirit world in nonphysical form. There's an exception to this rule, which is that sometimes we are specifically led to bring a much-needed energy to the planet and to humanity. When this happens, it's because their soul has integrated the spirit or divine aspect of themselves so wholly and fully that they have no more work to do on themselves.

Quintessences or Ascended Masters

I call souls who make that selfless choice "quintessence" souls or ascended masters. These brave beings incarnate into our dense, physical world just to help us in our own remembering process. They don't need to incarnate for their own growth anymore; they've finished their soul's development. These masters have transcended the lower vibration of fear while they were in human form. They only join us to bring in and anchor specific energies as a gift for the rest of us, and are we grateful when they do!

There are sub-levels within every soul level, even the quintessence soul level. Some examples of the highest and purest form of these souls are Jesus (who brought the energy of unconditional love) and Buddha (who brought the energy of compassion). More recently, Nelson Mandela crossed over into the light; he was a lower sub-level of quintessence soul that anchored the energy and thoughtform of forgiveness. These quintessences or masters will be covered in another book, but for now, just know that (thankfully) we always have at least a handful of these types on the planet at all times. It's one of those blessings that falls under the heading of Grace.

Same Sub, Different Periscope

Most of us are still in our soul's learning cycle. In that cycle, we'll eventually complete all five soul levels. The time it takes to complete your own soul's evolution is completely and entirely up to you. And while we all have unique experiences and personalities, these five levels look pretty similar in all of our lives. In some ways, these levels are a lot like our physical and neurological development. You'll discover the different and unique qualities of each level in the coming chapters, but let's look at some of the similarities.

Regardless of what soul level you're currently in, we all tend to wait until we're around age forty to fully engage all of the gifts and awareness that come with integrating our soul's development. (This is what I was referring to earlier when I mentioned a reactivation of the spiritual journey.) That's when most of us can really use what our soul has learned in previous incarnations— physically, neurologically, emotionally and spiritually. The perceptions and growth we embody within these five soul ages or phases are the same for all of us; the only differences are in how we experience them. Some of us gain access at a younger age, but it's not the norm.

We experience our lives through the lens of our soul. Where we are in the five-level blueprint dictates how we perceive ourselves, other living things, and the world in general. Just as a small child can't conceive of many grownup issues, a young soul will have trouble understanding an older soul's perspective. Older souls can lose patience with a younger soul, just like adults can have a hard time remembering what it was like to be a child, and can overlook the brightness or positive aspects inherent in that younger person.

We don't skip levels either. No jumping ahead! We can, however, move through our development with some conscious involvement. We can knowingly or unknowingly speed up or slow down our soul growth. We can motivate our forward progress with our thoughts and our willingness to expand our perceptions (our mind), and elevating our bodies by engaging in more light-producing activities to raise our personal frequency or vibration. At its most basic, when you're resonating at a high vibration, you feel positive and your soul is learning and growing. When the vibration or frequency is low, you feel emotionally heavy or negative, and soul-wise, you're not moving forward very smoothly or efficiently. This literally means that the higher your frequency, the more light you embody and the more you're developing your soul.

Your Free Will Includes Options

Not that most of us would consciously decide to do this, but we can also slow down our soul's evolution. Plenty of us do this without meaning to. How many times have you done something while you were thinking, "I really shouldn't be doing this" or "This doesn't feel right."? In those circumstances, we're resisting the opportunities that we've been given to grow. At that point, our personal vibration becomes lower and our soul's development slows.

~ ~ ~

What are some other ways that we get in our own way and slow our soul's growth? Anything we do that lowers our frequency can slow our soul's progress. Some examples would be:

- gossiping
- abusing the body with alcohol, drugs or low-vibration food (processed, chemical-laden food)
- complaining
- watching low-vibration media, like violent movies or constant news
- sarcasm
- perfectionism
- self-criticism
- judging others
- not getting enough sleep
- burning the candle at both ends
- breathing in toxins or chemicals, including synthetic fragrances, cigarette smoke, etc.
- chronic negative thinking
- surrounding ourselves with people who aren't supportive or positive

When we allow anything to get in the way of our natural evolution, it's called resistance, and while it may seem slow and inefficient, this resistance is also a necessary part of our overall growth process. We could also call it contrast.

We experience contrast when we create a situation in our lives that we don't really want or like. Through identifying what we don't like (the contrast), we learn what we really do want. It's an important tool. This process of resistance or contrast starts shortly after the soul is created (in the level one, "infant" soul realm), and it continues until we've completed every level of our soul's growth.

And so it begins—the inner turmoil and conflict with being in physical form that (until we reach higher levels of awareness) can plague us at the same time it connects us to every other human on the planet now, before, and after us. There is no human who has ever lived who hasn't experienced suffering on some level. Suffering, struggle, resistance (or contrast) is intended to be the catalyst for our soul's growth, strengthening our hearts and opening the door to our enlightenment—our inevitable, ultimate remembering. It's a necessary component in the overall scheme of things, so we might as well approach it with a grain of salt and more understanding.

Digging Your Heels In

Doesn't it seem pretty normal to react to a situation by feeling good or bad about it? On the outside, it does look like perfectly normal human behavior; you react to some external situation by feeling good or feeling bad, based on the external situation. If something I perceive as good happens, I feel good. If something I perceive as bad happens, I feel bad. While superficially that may not appear to be resistance, at its core, it is. On the surface, it looks like we're just going with the flow of life, reacting and responding "as directed" by life events. What we're really doing is going with the flow of external life, not the flow of our wise soul, our inner world.

Another approach is when we attempt to control every-thing that's happening in our macrocosmic world until we unwittingly create an unintended, compounding effect—the fear of spontaneity. Isn't it funny that we try to control our experience by using worry? It's as if we believe that, as long as we're worrying about this specific situation, we're keeping ourselves (or the person we're worrying about) safe. It makes no sense and it doesn't work, but it's ingrained in us until we are ready to release it.

At any given time, most people are engaged in one of these two unproductive methods. Right now, that's how the majority of folks on the planet live their lives: either feeling tossed about by circumstance or struggling for control at every turn. But on a true, deep soul level, that type of living is resisting who you really are. It's resistance to the natural state of oneness and growth and peace that we all have access to, every moment of every day, regardless of what's happening—good or bad. It's resisting connection with the real you, the "soul" you.

To be clear, it's normal, good and human for us to feel bad when something tragic happens. What's not normal is when we become so accustomed to feeling bad about that tragic event that we resist the natural lifting of our vibration, which provides us with relief from the bad feelings. In other words, if something painful happens, we feel bad. However, if we grab onto that bad feeling and start applying it anywhere and everywhere in our lives and don't allow the light of elevated perception to shine through, we're then in a state of resistance.

After some time passes from the initial tragic event, we could also allow ourselves to feel good and then, to avoid another painful time, attempt to control everything that happens from then on. This also is resistance. So yes, you can dig your heels in and resist your own growth, and at some point, it'll pile up on you. All of those little opportunities to raise your vibration that you ignored or fought against will take the shape of a big issue that will require you to rethink your ideas and perceptions about yourself, your situations, and everyone connected with you, and your soul will evolve.

We all have these barriers or overlays that are kind of like veils that are covering our true selves. These overlays come in the form of beliefs, thoughts, ideas, feelings, and patterns that we adopt from our family, culture, religion, environment, and society. The overlays reside within our energy field. We all hang onto them until we don't, until it's no longer working. You hold onto it until you get tired of feeling drained or anxious or creatively blocked, unhappy, self-critical, or any other of the long list of emotional and physical ailments that come along with holding energy that's not truly you.

Anytime you're feeling fear, anxiety or just plain bad, that's evidence of an overlay. When you're connected with your soul (i.e. you are connected with your authentic self), you feel good and peaceful, even if you're in the middle of suffering. At that point, you know that the suffering is bringing you one step deeper into love, healing and enlightenment.

There are only two types of feelings that we experience: love and fear (or in other words, allowing and resisting). If a feeling isn't love- and acceptance-based, it's fear. Imagine the example of a man who staunchly opposes the concept of a homosexual lifestyle for anyone he knows, and he believes it's just wrong. Maybe it's a religious belief, maybe it's cultural, but it's definitely fearful. Through our own life experiences, we're all offered many opportunities to raise our vibration and embody the natural acceptance that every soul will evolve to. In this example of the homophobic man, perhaps he'll start to see more positive references to homosexuality in the media. Then he might learn that one of his oldest friends (a role model he admires) or his favorite co-worker is homosexual.

These are all examples of opportunities to engage the soul's natural state of freedom, which includes accepting our own and other people's lifestyles without judgment. If his perceptions still don't start to clear up and start to resemble the soul's true state of freedom, then the big whammy comes. He learns that his adult child is homosexual. He loves him dearly, and to keep that treasured relationship, he must shift his perceptions. And just like that, he allows the energy of love to dissolve his fear. His frequency rises and he allows his soul's development to continue. Resistance is truly futile! Life will continue to present situations and people that will help us flex our muscles on a soul level. Every single situation in our lives is self-designed to help us grow.

Heading In The Right Direction

So how do we make sure we're moving forward at our perfect pace and growing consciously? We do this by actively and deliberately raising our frequency, and through that process, we enlighten our perception. When we increase our frequency and raise our vibration, we intentionally grow and develop our soul.

Shifting from judgment to discernment is an example of this. Judgment is making something or someone good or bad, right or wrong, in your mind. Elevate your frequency, relax into discernment, and it's no longer a question of good or bad, right or wrong. The questions become, "Is this right for me? Is this good for me?" This applies to situations that are all about you and those that have nothing to do with you.

For example, I have a family friend who has struggled with addiction to drugs and alcohol. It would make sense for me to say, "She shouldn't be doing that" or "That's bad," when she relapsed. The truth is that when she relapses, it's common for the family to experience fear. Those feelings are representing the energy of judgment, and it's not in alignment with the energy of the soul.

If I look at the same person, in the same situation, the first step in *my own* healing becomes acknowledging that I have fear around her issues—fear that she might ruin her life, someone else's, or die from her addiction. I can start to heal the fear by *talking to my soul self*, literally saying out loud *to myself*, "It makes perfect sense that you'd be fearful. I know how much you love her. I love you so much and I love your compassion. I love that you care so much..." and on and on. The idea is to overwhelm yourself with validation and love, completely taking the focus off of the person you're trying to control. When you feel validated, loved and accepted by yourself, then you can move into the next phase of healing, which we'll get to in the upcoming pages.

Any situation where you are attempting to control another person, whether it's through worry or taking tangible action, is a misunderstanding of your role. Your role is to hold the energy of unconditional love, fully understanding that you have no idea what experiences other people have agreed to and attracted to themselves in an effort to complete their own soul's development. Before each of us were born, we made those choices, and none of us are in a position to judge those experiences as "good" or "bad."

When I've overwhelmed myself with love and validation, I can then shift my perception from judging the situation or the person (thinking that something is bad) to discernment about her situation and my role (what she's doing wouldn't be what I would choose to do, wouldn't be good for me, and worrying about it isn't good for me, either). Obviously, it's exactly what she needs to experience right now for her soul to learn its valuable lessons, or it wouldn't be happening. No mistakes, no derailment, no unplanned disaster. It's an exercise for everyone involved.

~ ~ ~

How can you raise your frequency and consciously move forward in your soul's development to stay on track or accelerate your pace, if you choose to?

- Spending time in nature
- Praying
- Unplugging from modern life from time to time
- Dancing
- Meditation
- Hugging
- Doing something creative you can get lost in
- Caring for animals or people
- Gardening or farming
- Cooking or baking, if you love it
- Listening to or playing high-vibration music with a positive message
- Laughing
- Singing
- Feeding wildlife
- Camping or hiking
- Being in a positive community
- Self-care, such as massage, acupuncture, etc.
- Reading positive, spiritual literature, like you're doing in this moment!

If you've ever felt "blissed out" after getting a massage, doing yoga, praying, dancing, laughing, meditating, or being in nature, then you've experienced raising your frequency. It's usually a temporary state of feeling deeply that all is well. The point is that those short-lived "all is well" moments start to string together as your vibration increases, and your soul starts to get the hang of this whole growth, development, acceleration thing. As your frequency rises and becomes more stable, you hit a new reliable baseline of frequency/vibration, and now you've found yourself on a new level in your soul development.

You know that you're moving forward because your perception shifts, you feel more centered than you did before, happiness starts to feel more and more normal, and gratitude is much easier to come by. Your percentage of time spent in lower-vibration energies like worry, stress, attempts to control others, or self-criticism starts to be reduced. Your percentage of time spent in higher-vibration energies like harmony, love, and thankfulness starts to increase.

All Is Well

Enlightenment (or as I define it, perceiving reality accurately) is a state that feels more natural and more fulfilling than any other feeling you could ever feel. And on a deep soul level, because you know that it already exists for you, that it's within your reach, you're uncovering it within you; you are naturally evolving and gravitating toward that freedom. You'll have moments of enlightenment here and there, those indescribable "all is well" moments where you just don't have a care in the world. The coolest thing about all of this is that you don't have to seek it; it's going to happen, either way—maybe in this lifetime, maybe not, but it's inevitable. It's the natural evolution of the soul and it is intermingled with the energy of freedom every time. When you engage your awake, conscious mind in this process, you become more involved in your soul-life, which is where the fun is!

Lifetimes and Levels

Each of the five soul levels can take many incarnations to complete. Wouldn't it be great and super-efficient if we had one lifetime per level? We might sometimes wish that we could schedule it that way, but usually it takes many, many lifetimes per level. This isn't because we're slow learners, but because we have so much to learn and we learn it through so many different aspects. It's not just conceptual and perceptual learning; there is integration going on within every layer of your being. This includes all of the components of the subtle body, the mind, the physical body, the emotions... everything! Like many things worth having, this is an ongoing process.

How to Heal

When we address the manifestation of wounds in this lifetime, the healing reaches back into our previous incarnations, healing the origin of the issue. There are many different ways and modalities to heal. Here is a simple process of learning, healing and growing that really works. Pay close attention to steps 5–9.

1. **Contrast.** You experience something you don't like or want.

2. **Resistance.** You resist that experience by fighting with it emotionally, mentally, physically or spiritually. This manifests as complaining, feeling victimized by life, feeling depressed, anxious, worried, repressed, overwhelmed or triggered.

3. **Acceptance.** You accept the experience and start to look for the deeper meaning and truth. We get here through using techniques like journaling and meditation. Write it out and you'll become more calm and centered, and then move into Step 4.

4. **Allowing.** You allow your natural healing to begin, by seeing the experience for what it really is—a learning tool.

5. **Honoring.** Steps 5–9 are the most important action steps. Overwhelm yourself with validation, love and compassion regarding the experience. Talk to yourself aloud and say. "I love you so much. I understand why you feel the way you feel. It makes sense that you'd feel this way. I love you. I have so much compassion for you. I forgive you for anything and everything."

6. **Gratitude.** Give thanks for those "negative" feelings or energies or circumstances. Say, "Thank you, feelings of [name the feeling]. You're no longer needed in this body. You're no longer needed in my experience. Thank you. I've learned a lot. You've served me well.

Now your service is no longer needed."

7. **Breathe it out.** Take a deep breath in, Then, on a big exhale (while sensing the issues leaving you, flowing out through the bottoms of your feet) say, "All pain is now going back to Source. I release it. It is done. All is well." If your issue has to do with another person, you can take a deep breath and on the exhale, say, "I release you to your blessings, and I accept mine. It is done. All is well." When using this technique for relationships, you're not necessarily releasing the person from your experience; you might still have interaction with them. You get to choose whether or not you're going to continue the relationship. You're releasing the need within you to have some conflict with them, to feel minimized, abandoned, or whatever you've been feeling. Some part of you needed to feel those "negative" feelings in order to bring your attention to what was not yet healed and what needed unconditional love.

8. **Invitation.** Say, "I invite in the energies of love, peace, harmony, and prosperity (or whatever energies you're wanting to bring into your life or your body). Thank you, new energies!"

9. **Self-love.** It's now time to give yourself the energy that you were lacking in the painful situation. If you weren't feeling accepted by someone, work on self-acceptance. If you were raised in a troubled environment, create a peaceful space for yourself. If you

were being criticized by someone, catch yourself every time you criticize yourself and others, and replace it with praise.

10. **Truth.** Peace about the experience emerges, sometimes spontaneously, sometimes gradually.

11. **Perceiving reality accurately.** Enlightenment overtakes any and all perceived negativity about the contrast experience and healing has occurred.

12. **Stabilizing/Integration.** Your soul has taken another step forward on its evolutionary path. You will never repeat that experience or that particular form of contrast in exactly the same negative-feeling way.

Note: Using and re-using the tools in Steps 5–9 will start to streamline your healing and move you forward in ways you can't even imagine until you try it!

The levels of soul development aren't sharply defined from level to level. There are some overlap lifetimes, where you can have one foot in a baby soul lifetime and one foot in the next level, or you're in a mature lifetime but almost in the old soul level. We sometimes even choose to have a lifetime where we mostly "coast"; soul-wise, we're not making great strides and that's okay. Your free will is more important that any efficiency could ever be. Whether consciously or subconsciously, you are choosing the rate of your soul's growth. You are sovereign in your own life and in soul terms, you have the free will to choose every aspect of what you experience.

Mother Earth

I'm not an expert on what's happening scientifically with the Earth's magnetism and frequency, but I am aware that the Earth is naturally accelerating, raising her frequency. As an electromagnetic human being, you're sensitive to the electromagnetic frequency of the planet you inhabit. As the Earth's frequency rises, we are all adapting by raising our own personal frequency. The raising of our frequency helps our soul to develop by crowding out the lower, less pure energies.

On a spiritual level, I can assure you that the quickening that's underway on our planet is absolutely a helpful, supportive development that is energetically spurring us onward and upward. We are no longer like salmon swimming upstream. For hundreds—if not thousands—of years, humans were struggling to grow, soul-wise. The frequency of the planet was low, and so was ours. Now, we are learning to go with the flow of high-frequency energy and we can ride this wave as long as we choose to. This is an integral aspect of the development of our individual souls, because we incarnate into these earthly lifetimes for the main purpose of soul development, so that we will eventually achieve enlightenment.

~ ~ ~

Why would we choose to incarnate at this particular time in history?

- The frequency of the earth is helping us energetically and spiritually evolve.
- We have computers to hold the data that we no longer need to keep in our own memory banks, so this frees us up to use our minds to innovate like never before.
- Older souls want to help the younger ones.
- Those who are caregivers of the earth want to help heal the environment.
- There are tremendous strides to witness and assist in, regarding harmony among races and other perceived divisions among humans and other living things.
- We have tangible proof (through science and technology) that every thought affects every living thing.

We've Got Help

Remembering that you chose your parents, what part of the world you'd be born in, how you would look, your natural gifts and skills, and your goals for your soul's evolution, and you didn't figure all of that out by yourself. You made those decisions with the help and guidance of your divine team, which includes your spirit guides, guardian angels, ascended masters and some close members of your soul family.

Let's briefly define each of these helpers, starting with your guides in spirit. We all have spirit guides. They are human beings who have passed out of physical form and continue to live on the other side, in the spirit world.

You and your guides have been connected since before you were born, in your life between lives. You mutually agreed to have this relationship. Your guides agreed to be with you, literally guiding you through the challenges of life, ensuring that you're getting every opportunity to heal and reach the goals you have set for your soul's growth. Typically, we don't know our guides from this lifetime, which means they aren't our deceased family members or friends. Only very rarely would that be the case.

We also all have guardian angels, who are a different species altogether. Unlike spirit guides, there are no human beings who are angels. Your grandmother may have been angelic to you in this lifetime, but she's not going to turn into an actual angel when she crosses over to the other side. Our loved ones certainly look out for us, and they can help us in a variety of ways, but technically, they're not angels.

Many loved ones are members of your soul family, and will remain connected with you, no matter what. Your soul family consists of the main people that you've been incarnating with again and again. You know when you meet someone in your soul family, because you very quickly feel like you've known that person forever and, on a soul level, you may have. There's a magnetism there that's unlike any other relationship.

When someone in our soul family is in the spirit world, the help we get from them comes not just from the love we feel or the love they feel, but it's also just inherent in the connection. We all want to help each other. This applies even if you didn't perceive them as helpful when they were here in physical form. They could've been providing a painful situation (contrast) for your spiritual and emotional growth.

All of us also consult with the highest council of light before we incarnate, so we can know we're following our most benevolent path. The council of light includes beings who are in non-physical form in the spirit world. They are dedicated to our spiritual evolution and embodiment of light.

From this perspective, it stands to reason that there is nothing in this life that happens to you that is not actually for you. You agreed to learn the specific lessons you need to learn to move through whatever soul level you are in, and it takes some patience and understanding to really accept that not only does everything happen for a reason, but on a deep, soul level, we already know what that reason is.

The reason is our soul's progression, through the raising of our personal and collective frequencies. That's it! No more searching for the mysterious, vague answer to the question, "Why am I here?" You are here to elevate yourself on a soul level, and in doing so, experience joy and love and every other wonderful energy that this life has to offer. All things happen for the purpose of helping us along on own spiritual journey. We all have individual and group missions (or service commitments) that support our soul's elevation, but in the bigger picture, we're all here for the same general reason.

Your Intentions as We Forge Ahead

As you move forward in this book and explore the levels of your soul's development, you're going to be opening up to your own healing, more and more. On that note, I have three intentions for you to consider. Before you read further, setting these intentions will help you get the most out of this book, so if these resonate with you, go ahead and say them aloud before you go on to the next chapter.

The first intention is, "I intend to seek to understand and accept all living beings as they are." There's a phrase within the prayer of Saint Francis that reads, "O Divine Master, grant that I may not so much seek to be consoled as to console; to be understood as to understand." In his book, *The Seven Habits of Highly Effective People*, Steven Covey rephrases this truth into a simple sentence: "Seek first to understand, then to be understood."

This is the origin of our first intention—one that will change your life in so many positive ways if you apply it across the board, and not just to the reading of this book. In my own life, adopting that intention has changed all of my relationships for the better, in more ways than I can express here. Since we've all already been through at least one of these soul levels and we'll all eventually experience every level, it makes sense that—through understanding and awareness of these soul levels—we could allow each person to experience their lives without incurring judgment or criticism from us.

There will always be people in the world who are younger souls than you are. There will always be older souls, as well. Your job includes accepting where you are in your own personal process, and then accepting where others are in their process, too. Remember, the soul's natural state is freedom and we're all working our way back to that freedom, integrated with "perceiving reality accurately," without fear.

Maybe you're not having "just a difference of opinion" with a family member. Maybe the people in the opposing political party aren't ignorant. Maybe your neighbor who's addicted to drama isn't really crazy. Perhaps the spiritual teacher who speaks about things you just don't get isn't delusional. It's their soul's age. It's normal and wonderful and perfectly acceptable that we are all thrown together at different stages like an all-ages, one-room schoolhouse. It can look like chaos or it can look like fun, and either way, it's an exercise. It's not only safe, but it's natural to relax into our own journey and not judge others for what theirs looks like, because if you haven't already been where they are soul-wise, you surely will be one day.

"A fundamental conclusion of the new physics also acknowledges that the observer creates the reality. As observers, we are personally involved with the creation of

our own reality. Physicists are being forced to admit that the universe is a 'mental' construction. Pioneering physicist Sir James Jeans wrote: 'The stream of knowledge is heading toward a non-mechanical reality; the universe begins to look more like a great thought than like a great machine. Mind no longer appears to be an accidental intruder into the realm of matter, we ought rather hail it as the creator and governor of the realm of matter. Get over it, and accept the inarguable conclusion. The universe is immaterial-mental and spiritual.' ~ R. C. Henry, Professor of Physics and Astronomy at Johns Hopkins University[1]

The second intention I'm asking you to consider is, "I intend to identify and heal all that is unresolved within me; I allow myself to heal." When you're an older soul, you're working on healing yourself in a different way than the other soul ages. You're healing deeply and not just from this lifetime; you're healing from any unhealed aspects from any other lifetime, as well. This means that as you read on in this book, you'll see an aspect of yourself in the description of every soul level that you learn about. You'll identify something within that soul level that feels like you. Your unhealed parts are coming to your attention to be healed, and it takes a genuine commitment to your own well-being to follow through on that path. If you're willing to take the plunge, go ahead now and say the second

1. "The Mental Universe", *Nature* 436:29, 2005, R. C. Henry, Professor of Physics and Astronomy at Johns Hopkins University

intention out loud, with some feeling, like you mean it! "I intend to identify and heal all that is unresolved within me; I allow myself to heal."

This brings us to our third and final intention: your mission, so to speak, if you choose to accept it. The third intention is "I intend to trust the process of life; all is well." This is the most important of the three, and the most life-changing. That's what this book is really about—the process of life: why things happen, why we feel hurt, why things are so hard sometimes, and how we can make life better.

Most of us have some level of anxiety or depression or inner chaos until we are willing to trust that this life is a co-creation, a partnership between each of us individually and our Divine Source. We then include our team of guides and angels and loved ones and soul family, and we're off to the races.

When you're open to your own soul, life opens up as well, and it's never the same. You're not just trying to get through it, making the best of whatever comes your way. You're no longer just searching for the silver lining when things are weird, painful or scary. *Instead of looking for the light in dark situations, you BECOME the light in EVERY situation.* You're truly awake and aware of all of life's exercises that are helping you grow, and you're naturally grateful for the magic of this life. So now, put your heart in it, and say, "I intend to trust the process of life; all is well."

In the following chapters, you're going to learn all about

the different soul levels, and you'll have an opportunity to heal those aspects of you, from the time when you were a younger soul. This is an imperative step in your soul's growth, and I'm honored to guide you in that process. So as you read further, remember that you'll recognize other people in your life (or in the public arena) who fit the description of the younger soul levels, and you'll likely see aspects of yourself, as well. It's a beautiful process when you allow it to flow through you. As you read these pages, you're receiving energy healing transmissions that will help you along the way, and you can take personal responsibility for your own healing by doing the meditations and techniques at the end of each chapter.

To your healing!

Intentions

I intend to seek to understand and accept all living beings.

I intend to identify and heal all that is unresolved within me; I allow myself to heal.

I intend to trust the process of life; all is well.

Affirmations

What's the deal with affirmations?

"Any idea, plan, or purpose may be placed in the mind through repetition of thought." ~ Napoleon Hill

Positive affirmations are phrases that are repeated to help you integrate thoughts or beliefs that will increase your happiness, health, or joy. The repetition helps you upgrade your beliefs, affecting every aspect of your life, in a positive way. Every thought that you habitually think becomes an affirmation, whether it's positive and life-affirming, or a complaint that builds resentment, victim thinking, or negative feelings.

Studies have now proven that people who repeat positive affirmations reduce stress and are able to shift their thinking through repetition.[2] Start by repeating one of the phrases here about ten or twenty times, and see how you feel. You'll feel uplifted and, as affirmations become part of your daily routine, you'll likely notice more and more improvement in your overall mindset.

I like to post affirmations on my desk at work or on the bathroom mirror, so I'll see them every day. Just change them out when you feel like you've gotten the upgrade you needed, which is when you really, truly believe the positive thought!

---

2. *Psychology Today*, May 5, 2013. Research from Carnegie Mellon University.

Affirm:

My true nature is light and I look for the light in all beings.

I easily and naturally see the true essence of everyone I encounter.

It's safe for me to release resistance and allow my soul to lead.

I raise my vibration to the highest and most beneficial vibration for me.

"Your role is to hold the energy of unconditional love, fully understanding that you have no idea what experiences other people have agreed to and attracted to themselves in an effort to complete their own soul's development."

~ CHAPTER 2 ~

THE KARMA MYTH & THE CHAKRAS

BY THIS POINT, YOU'VE PROBABLY GOTTEN THE IDEA that we choose our experiences, and that anything and everything that happens in this lifetime springs from an effort and a desire for your soul to develop and heal. This brings us to what I call "The Karma Myth." The Karma Myth is the widely-held belief that when painful things happen in our lives, it's punishment for something we've done in this lifetime or in a previous incarnation. It's summed up in the oft-spoken "What goes around, comes around."

It's important to understand karma clearly before moving forward in this book. The higher-level truth of karma is that you have issues that are unhealed and unresolved from previous incarnations that manifest as issues in this lifetime. It means the same to say that you have issues that are unhealed and unresolved from your previous soul phases. Everything painful or unwanted that happens in this life is a reminder to you that you have an unhealed wound from another time, either from this incarnation or another.

These soul-level, energetic wounds present themselves in this life as illnesses, physical problems, emotional traumas, accidents, difficult relationships, money problems, addictions, anxiety, depression, weight issues, and on and on. Anything that draws your attention to what needs to be healed within you and your subtle body is a karmic wound, from this or another lifetime.

If you never again thought another self-critical thought, judged someone else, or ever withheld love because of your own fear, then you would be connected with your true, authentic soul-self and you wouldn't be creating any more karmic issues to heal and clear up later. This is how the cycle continues and how we either create or clear karma with every thought, action and word. It's self-defeating to try to be perfect or police your own thoughts or judge yourself for being, feeling and acting like a human being. That attitude creates the energy of self-betrayal and creates more karma, due to the absence of self-love and self-acceptance. Over time, the idea is to relax into your true nature, where it's natural for you to feel good; to love yourself, others, and the world; and be filled with gratitude for the opportunity to be here on Earth with the rest of us, learning together and healing together. Remember, it's an exercise.

That is karma. When we truly understand karma, it's so natural and easy to feel grateful for everything that comes our way in this life, even if it's painful or confusing. What feels good, what feels bad—it's all helpful information that's intended to guide us on our journey into our natural state of enlightenment. When you heal these issues on a soul-level in this lifetime, you've not only healed yourself of your current life issue, but you've also healed the *origin* of the problem; you've cleaned up what has been preventing you from achieving more enlightenment, or perceiving reality accurately.

Think of it like a physical issue. You experience a symptom like a fever. It doesn't feel good, but it's not personal; it's not punishment. It's your body using all of its divine wisdom to heat the body to destroy a pathogen that can't live at that higher temperature. The discomfort is part of the healing, and it's completely natural. Thank God for these natural processes! You don't have to be mentally aware of the existence of the pathogen or what type it is, in order for your body to handle it naturally. Your mind (consciousness) doesn't even have to be involved.

Karma is the accumulation of soul-wounds that you want to heal, even if you're not consciously aware of them. Your soul has been through multiple lifetimes, and through that incarnation cycle, you've been growing through a process of soul-growth-phases. Anything that wasn't healed from any previous lifetime or soul phase must be healed, for you to begin to experience the phases of enlightenment. Those soul wounds are stored in the subtle body system, specifically in the chakra system. For reminders of a good step-by-step healing process to start with, refer to the "How to Heal" section in Chapter One.

So how do we move into the next soul phase, if we still have unhealed stuff from our earlier phase? These phases don't have clear-cut edges; they blend into each other. The "graduation" from one soul phase to the next happens when your awareness has expanded to a specific point while your frequency rises to a higher level, not necessarily when you've healed everything associated with it.

What about the good things in our lives, the gifts and blessings? Are those karma, too? Yes! But instead of reminders of unhealed wounds, the blessings are the reminders of areas that have been healed, the work has been done. Blessings and gifts are the evidence of times when you've remembered your true nature, when you've been willing to acknowledge and honor that God-spark within you.

Chakras and Soul Age

Before we get into the first level souls, I want you to have some basic information about chakras, so that the following chapters will fall into place easily for you.

There is a direct attachment from our chakras to our soul, and this connection is an important part of all of us. The chakras are the energy centers of the body, in the form of swirling vortices of light energy. We have hundreds of chakras, but only seven main ones that we'll address here. You'll see more detail on the chakras in the following chapters, but here are the most important things to know at this point.

1. Each chakra is a receiver and a transmitter of energy, including thoughts, feelings, beliefs, patterns and more.

2. Each chakra also has a blueprint of its own that carries the dynamic energy of that particular chakra.

3. Our physical and emotional health are affected by the health and vitality of our chakras, and vice versa.

4. We receive light energy that is stepped down from Source into our chakras; it enters us through the crown chakra of our head. This is our connection to our spirit and our Source.

5. We receive Earth energy from the planet through the root chakra, at the base of the spine. This is our connection to the planet and to our ability to survive physically.

6. Our chakras hold our unhealed karmic issues in different levels, with specific wounds presenting at specific times, as we discover and peel away the layers of our wounding.

You can see how important these energy centers are, even if you only have this brief knowledge of them. The seven main chakras are located in a vertical row from the base of the spine (at the tailbone), all the way up to the crown of the head. In order from the bottom up, they are:

1. the Root Chakra, at the base of the spine;
2. the Sacral Chakra, in the lower abdomen, just below the navel;
3. the Solar Plexus Chakra, just above the navel in the upper abdomen;
4. the Heart Chakra, in the center of the chest;
5. the Throat Chakra, in the throat area;
6. the Brow Chakra, on the forehead, in between and above the eyes; and
7. the Crown Chakra, centered just above the head.

At the bottom of the stack, the root chakra extends like a vortex of energy from the base of the spine down toward the knees; at the top, the crown chakra extends from the middle of the brain up through the top of the skull and connects to the higher levels from there. All of the other chakras extend toward the front of the body in a vortex. A vortex also extends behind the back as well. So each chakra (except the root and the crown) actually has two vortices of energy included within it, like two horizontal cones connected to each other at their tips.

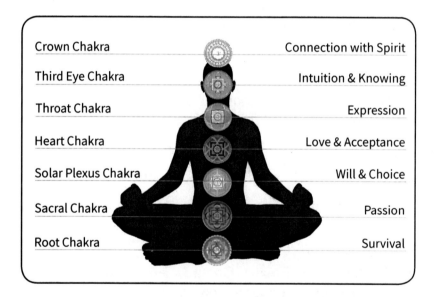

Crown Chakra	Connection with Spirit
Third Eye Chakra	Intuition & Knowing
Throat Chakra	Expression
Heart Chakra	Love & Acceptance
Solar Plexus Chakra	Will & Choice
Sacral Chakra	Passion
Root Chakra	Survival

Depending on your soul's age, you will naturally be viewing the world through the lens of a specific chakra or group of chakras, and you will be clearing out the overlays or barriers that exist in that chakra or group of chakras until you graduate to the next level of your soul's development. Your entire life, you'll be experiencing yourself and the world around you from the perspective of one or more specific, pre-determined chakras. Each soul level is motivated by that specific chakra or group of chakras. This means that everyone on that soul level has that chakra development or theme in common, among other things. We'll explore this more deeply in the following chapters.

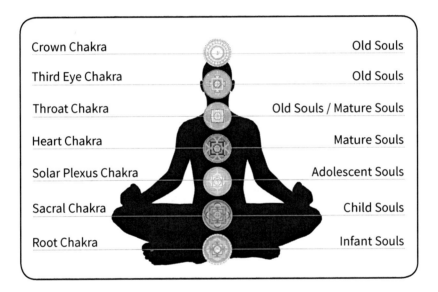

Crown Chakra	Old Souls
Third Eye Chakra	Old Souls
Throat Chakra	Old Souls / Mature Souls
Heart Chakra	Mature Souls
Solar Plexus Chakra	Adolescent Souls
Sacral Chakra	Child Souls
Root Chakra	Infant Souls

Soul Levels, Chakra Development, and Focus

- Infant Souls: Root (Survival)
- Child Souls: Root and Sacral (Survival, Passion and Creation)
- Adolescent Souls: Root, Sacral and Solar Plexus (Survival, Passion and Creation, Will and Choice)
- Mature Souls: Root, Sacral, Solar Plexus, and Heart (Survival, Passion and Creation, Will and Choice, Love and Acceptance)

- Old Souls: Root, Sacral, Solar Plexus, Heart, Throat, Third Eye and Crown (Survival, Passion and Creation, Will and Choice, Love and Acceptance, Expression, Intuition and Knowing, Connection with Spirit)

Just to make things even more interesting, at the same time that your soul is perceiving life through a chakra-tinted lens, you're also going through normal human chakra development at specific, physical-age-related intervals. This means that whether you're an infant soul or an old soul, in every lifetime you're developing your chakras during specific physical-age cycles. So in every lifetime, when you're 13 years old, you're working with the sacral chakra energy of passion and creativity, and when you're 40, you're activating your brow chakra, developing your intuition and learning how to trust yourself. You'll receive lessons during those age ranges that will help to hone those specific chakras and their correlating energies. This is important to know as you begin to heal from any situation or circumstance where you felt wounded, unimportant, minimized, or just in pain. When we understand the cycles of development from a subtle body, energetic perspective, self-understanding and awareness increase and self-love and compassion become easier and easier.

For example, when I was 30 years old, I was in a relationship where I felt like I had no voice. When I expressed myself from my heart, it wasn't received well. So, like many people with underdeveloped throat chakras, I withdrew. I decided that I would rather keep the peace than express myself and deal with the emotionally-upsetting consequences. This relationship continued to teach me for quite a while, as I realized more and more that I wasn't going to be satisfied with being withdrawn and not speaking my truth. I had many physical throat and neck issues that popped up during that time, as reminders that my throat chakra wasn't getting the attention that it needed.

After a while, because I had the natural growth cycle of the throat chakra to work with at that physical age, I realized that the reason that the relationship was presented to me was to help me notice what I needed to do for myself. I needed to flex the muscles of the throat chakra, and learn how to speak my truth, regardless of the consequences, perceived or real. How the information I expressed was received wasn't my business. When I embarked on healing that area, by expressing myself and giving myself lots of support during that time, I was able to improve my situation dramatically. And no, the relationship didn't continue forever, but we both learned so much!

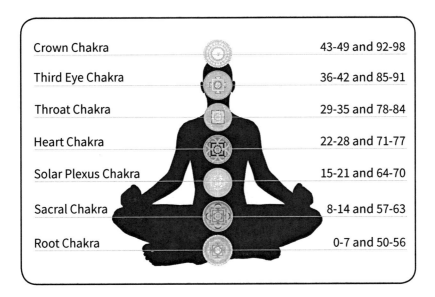

Crown Chakra	43-49 and 92-98
Third Eye Chakra	36-42 and 85-91
Throat Chakra	29-35 and 78-84
Heart Chakra	22-28 and 71-77
Solar Plexus Chakra	15-21 and 64-70
Sacral Chakra	8-14 and 57-63
Root Chakra	0-7 and 50-56

Releasing Non-Beneficial Beliefs

It's important to remember that every soul level (infant, child, adolescent, mature, old and even the quintessence level) has several sub-levels within that phase. Let's use the example of an old soul. Every old soul won't be in the same phase at the same time, so remember that as you read this book and recognize how you're feeling about your life. Old souls who are new to the old soul phase can seem frustrated and weary of life, while old souls who are nearing the end of this soul phase are brimming with enthusiasm and excitement about just being here and serving and loving and enjoying the planet. The process from weary to enthusiastic is an incredible journey of healing old wounds and clearing out any energies, beliefs, or thoughtforms that are no longer serving you.

Following are some examples of energies that you'll be healing and clearing out: from the root chakra, the belief that money is the root of all evil; from the sacral chakra, that you're a victim because someone did something horrible to you; or from the solar plexus chakra, that you'll never be fulfilled because life just isn't that way. We all carry energies, beliefs and thoughtforms that that we have absorbed and claimed because of our life experiences, but are not the highest level of truth. We hold these energies and live through them by default, until it no longer works for us and we release them. This is where the true freedom comes from! Can you imagine yourself just feeling free all the time? It is possible; you are on your way.

~ ~ ~

Sensory Experience: Think back in your mind to a time when you felt as free as you can remember. Maybe it's a childhood memory, maybe it's a great vacation you took recently, or maybe it's when you were in college and had a weekend off, with absolutely nothing to do except what you wanted to do. For me, it's when I was riding my bike when I was a kid. The wind in my hair, no one expecting me to be anywhere, no responsibilities, no schedule, no planned route. Just being outside and riding for riding's sake. If you don't have a memory that does it for you, then imagine what freedom would look like for you, or you can write the word "freedom" on a piece of paper in front of you.

The next step is for you to touch your thumb to your index finger, on each hand, in a meditative hand mudra position. Hold that hand position for the rest of this exercise. Now think of that memory or thought, and let yourself daydream it until it's so real that you can really *feel* it. You feel how you felt when you were riding your bike, or laying on the beach, or hiking in a canyon, or dancing—whatever it is. Let yourself feel the wind or the sun and the unmistakable feeling inside of liberation. Take some deep breaths and let the feeling permeate your entire being. Enjoy the feeling as long as you like.

When you're complete with this, remember that you can go back to that feeling at any moment, and the more often you do, the easier this journey will be. You've reminded yourself that your soul's natural state is freedom, and that you already know how to do this. You're just going to expand that state from being a moment in a daydream, to being the way you live your life from day to day. You're going to allow that feeling to become your new normal. You're on your way to remembering your soul. When you need a reminder, put your fingers in that meditative hand mudra position and start to build the positive energy of that memory.

If you feel like you're an old soul, in the fifth level of development, why is it important to know about the four, younger soul levels? Wouldn't it make more sense to just learn about old souls, so you can know yourself better?

There are three main reasons that it's important to know about the other soul phases. First, you are interacting every day with people who are at different soul levels than you are, and it's easy for an older soul to get aggravated or frustrated when dealing with younger souls. It's an integral part of your own soul's development to transform that frustration into compassion and understanding. When you—on some level—accept that you have gone through the same phase that is a trigger for you in other people, you release your frustration and can become a more healed, authentic version of yourself. It's like an older sibling getting annoyed with a younger one, but when they remember when they were going through that same phase, the annoyance can turn into guidance.

The second reason is that the older soul personality

can become isolated as they age, if they don't understand their place in the world. Have you ever felt like you just weren't understood by anyone around you? Or that you were the only calm or sane person in the room or in your family? Older souls have these experiences and can feel upset by not being accepted by the younger souls around them. As you learn more and more about the other soul phases, you'll require acceptance from them less and less. You'll see how you can serve others and yourself, in the most loving and effective way. You'll know where you fit and how to move forward. It's part of your path of spiritual awakening.

The third reason is that every issue that comes up in your life is connected with a chakra. As you've learned, every chakra is connected with a soul age or level and a physical age, as well. You picked up this book because you're ready to see your problems as challenges that are indicating that something is unresolved and needs attention on an energetic, spiritual level, rather than continuing to believe that problems are just problems. This shift requires that we address our issues and wounds intellectually, emotionally, spiritually and sometimes physically, while recognizing that the core of every challenge is in its energy.

When you have challenges that are survival-related, such as financial issues, chronic health conditions, or trauma from a scary "life or death" experience, they are considered a root chakra issue, which is also a level one, infant soul issue. This means two important things: one, every survival-related challenge that has come up in your life is just relaying information from an unresolved or unhealed wound from when you were a very young, infant soul; and two, those survival-related challenges first showed up in this lifetime, between the time you were in utero and age seven. The issues could come up at any age, but the "in this life" origin would be when you were little. Every challenge has these two aspects. If you didn't have some wounding from your lifetimes as an infant soul, then you wouldn't have survival-related issues in this lifetime, as a very young child or continuing into adulthood.

These two aspects are inextricably linked and when we heal the origin (the wounds/healing opportunities from lifetimes as a new, infant soul), the early-onset symptoms (the issues that showed up for you as a child in *this* lifetime), and the late-stage symptoms (the problems you are having now), then the overall issues become resolved and disappear. We know that addressing both the origin and the symptom has a healing ripple effect that resonates throughout all of our past lifetimes up to and through today. Reading this book and doing the steps in the "How to Heal" section of Chapter One, along with the exercises included at the end of each chapter, will help facilitate this multi-dimensional healing.

Those of us who are mature and old souls have agreed to heal as much as we possibly can in this lifetime. When you're an older soul, you're given the opportunity to heal yourself on every level, and in so many ways. We all have issues in our lives, whether it's physical, emotional, mental, spiritual, or a combination of all of those. The only reason why you have any unresolved issues at all is because they are coming up to be healed. *Every unresolved issue, even an illness, is **information**, not affliction.* When you address problems as information and not affliction, you can approach every challenge that comes up as an opportunity to become more and more your authentic self. This is the goal. The energy of enlightenment isn't just reserved for how we perceive the outside world. It is, at its most basic, how we perceive our self. We want to fully realize our self, so we can be that authentic version that is waiting (just under the surface) to be revealed and honored.

Learning about the other soul levels means learning about yourself.

As you read the following chapters, you're going to see aspects of yourself (at least a little) in each soul level. The majority of the traits in the first few soul levels most likely won't apply *directly* to you, but you'll have bits and pieces that ring true for you. If those specifics that resonate with you are considered "negative" or non-beneficial, then those are the areas where you have some unhealed issues from when you were in that soul phase. If the specifics that resonate with you are the "positive," beneficial aspects, then you're connecting with the healed aspects of you, with regard to your own experiences in that soul age. Let's look at some examples, because this is super important to fully understand before we move forward.

If you have trouble finishing projects, that's an issue with the solar plexus chakra, which originated when you were a level three soul, an adolescent soul. The origin of your habit of not completing projects will be something that happened when you were in that third level of soul development. Maybe in some past lifetime, you finished a project (such as building your house) and then you died? Or maybe in another lifetime, every time you completed a project, you never got credit for it, or it was rejected by an authority figure? If so, it makes sense that you hold some natural resistance to completing projects in this lifetime. If that issue remains unresolved, the majority of your symptoms (i.e. not completing projects) will show up in this lifetime between the ages of 15-21 and 64-70, because those are the physical age cycles for the solar plexus chakra.

When you heal your past lifetime experience through compassion and love for yourself as you were in that phase and for others who are in that same soul phase, and you also address the issue in this current lifetime, you will no longer have the habit of not completing projects.

This same scenario applies to physical issues. For example, when I was a child I had frequent, painful bladder infections that seemed to have no obvious cause. Bladder is a root chakra organ, so the reason that the infections were coming up was because there was something that was not healed from when I was a level one infant soul. Remember it's not an affliction; it's information. The physical healing process may start out the same—with a doctor visit and medication—but the way to stop the cycle of those infections coming up again and again, is to heal the energy in the root chakra. Somewhere in my past life experience, I had some abuse that scarred that chakra. So in this lifetime, to make sure that I gave that area some healing attention, my body was prone to infection in that area.

I first felt frustrated and victimized, by my body and by life in general. Once I got over the frustration and feelings of victimization about the infections, and just gave myself lots of love and encouragement, the pattern was interrupted and eventually stopped. Obviously, I had felt frustrated and victimized in that previous lifetime, and through meditation I discovered the actual past life memory of the abuse and my reaction to it. But even if I hadn't recalled an actual past life memory, even if I couldn't consciously access that information, my chakras remembered the feelings and allowed something physical to represent that energy. This was to give me another chance to fill my body, mind and spirit with unconditional love, and I'll give you some tools at the end of the following chapters to help you achieve the same thing.

So let's say you live in the modern world, but you have a natural affinity for an indigenous culture. You love the artistry, the connection with the Earth, the traditions and the tribal society. You do what you can to help support the efforts of tribal people by contributing to nonprofits or buying fair trade goods. This type of connection indicates that there's a part of you that feels good about the time when you were in a tribal culture, when you were an infant soul, brand new to the planet. It was probably a good experience for you. If it wasn't, then somewhere along the way, you've healed your outstanding issues from that time, the root chakra time. It would stand to reason, as well, that you would have a pretty smooth experience in this lifetime between birth and age 7 and between the ages 50–56, because that's the time the root chakra is in full development mode in our current physical existence.

How cool is it that you don't have to be psychic and know every past life experience that isn't healed, and that you don't have to have all of the facts, in order to move forward on your soul's journey? Your energy field and your chakras hold all of those memories for you. Then the chakras project that energy onto your emotions, your mind and sometimes your physical body, all so you can have another chance to heal the deepest wounds that your soul has ever encountered. Your body and mind agree to accept that painful energy, because every aspect of you is always in agreement on one thing: you want to be healed.

Allowing yourself to be healed is the next hurdle, as you'll remember from the previous chapter. Resistance is common, but as they say, futile. Your body and mind will keep giving you all sorts of opportunities to heal—from recurring thought patterns, to physical issues to emotional problems—to draw your attention to what's unresolved and to give you the gift of information so that you can truly, deeply heal. Your freedom is right around the corner.

The following tools and techniques are to help you heal and to help your soul grow. There are many ways to achieve those goals, but these are some of my favorites. You can use these techniques anywhere, anytime, and they require very little effort. Your desire to heal and the willingness to take a few steps are all you need.

Affirmations

I allow myself to heal.

It's safe for me to heal.

It's safe for me to relax.

Centering

Read the instructions in this paragraph, then stand up, close your eyes and do this centering exercise.

Instructions: Let your hands hang loosely by your sides. You're going to make a figure eight movement with your body. Shift your weight from one foot to the other as you make a figure eight with your hips. You can close your eyes and take some deep breaths. Let your exhale be audible. Now let your arms move with your body in that figure eight pattern. Anytime you're ever feeling out of sorts, or nervous, or anxious, or tired, make this movement with your body. Your body knows this is a natural movement of your cells and energy field. Continue to make the figure eight movement for 1–2 minutes or as long as you like.

Mantras

A mantra is a word or phrase that's repeated many times, over and over, for spiritual awakening, healing and self-realization. Although traditionalists will repeat mantras 108 times, you may repeat a mantra just a few times, or as many times as you like. Different mantras have different meanings and different effects. I like to repeat mantras in a language other than my native English, so my conscious mind cannot argue with the idea or the energy that I'm cultivating. The vibration of mantra sounds is medicine to your energy body, your mind and your soul.

The mantra that will be helpful for you at this time (and that will continue to be helpful throughout your spiritual journey) is the word "Om" or "Aum". This mantra is the sound of all creation and is a sacred syllable that spans time and space. It's a grounding sound, while also expansive and liberating. If you're willing to repeat the sound for several minutes, your chakras will feel balanced and harmonized, and your mind will relax.

You'll be amazed at how you feel after you've repeated the sound, especially if you choose to incorporate the following mudra at the same time. I've heard "om" called "the great cosmic YES!" and that's appropriate for how you'll feel after repeating or chanting it. There are some beautiful recordings available, if you choose to follow along with some music and chanting.

When repeating mantras, take in a deep breath, and then on the exhale, repeat the mantra. In the case of "Om," the sound is a gradual fusion of three syllables, AW – OO – MMM, gliding from one syllable to the next. Let the "AW-OO" part of the syllables drag out for a few seconds, and then let the "MMM" sound drag on for several seconds. You'll be sure to feel the vibration if you're holding the sound this way. Your mind, body, soul and spirit will thank you if you're willing to try some mantras. It's amazing how simple and at the same time, life-changing, mantras can be. There's a reason why they've stood the test of time, being repeated throughout the ages in almost every society.

Mudras

All over the world, in many cultures since ancient times, specific yogic hand positions and gestures have been used for healing and spiritual growth. In Sanskrit, the word *mudra* means "gesture" or "seal." Mudras are used to connect with the universal energy and to connect with the Divine spark within ourselves. Holding your fingers and hands in the mudras will stimulate higher levels of awareness and self-realization, and activate mechanisms of self-healing and the flow of vital energy (prana or chi). Anyone can practice using hand mudras, regardless of age, skill level or understanding of yoga practice.

You'll see hand mudras at the end of each chapter with specific instructions and descriptions, as one part of the healing process. Be patient with yourself when it comes to mudras. The hand positions can feel clumsy at first and can be hard to hold for very long. For each mudra, you'll see a recommended length of time, but only hold the position for as long as it feels comfortable.

Bhairava Mudra

Benefits: Allows relaxation, calms the mind, helpful in meditation.

Technique: Place right hand on top of the left, rest both hands in the lap, palms up. Keep your fingers gently together, including the thumbs. You can also put the left hand on top of the right, for the alternate Divine feminine version of this mudra. Use whichever version feels most natural to you.

Hold your hands in your lap, breathe deeply, and hold for 5 to 30 minutes, incorporating a mantra or an affirmation from this chapter, if you like.

(see image on next page)

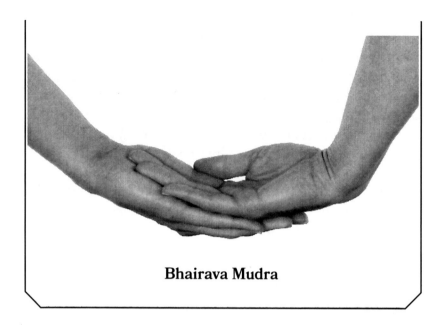

Bhairava Mudra

Guided Meditation to Allow My Healing

Be seated comfortably, and breathe in a relaxed way. You're entering into this meditation with full heart engagement. Affirm out loud or silently three times: "I allow myself to heal. I allow myself to heal. I allow myself to heal." Take a deep breath and let that energy settle in. You've already changed your chemistry, you've changed your hormones, and you've changed your energy field, just from repeating that phrase.

All you have to do for the next few minutes is just relax and remember to breathe. I'll be reminding you, but if you catch yourself holding your breath, remember that it's time to breathe. Go ahead and just close your eyes, relax, and take a few deep breaths (deeper than usual). Exhale any tension, and then you can go ahead and return your breathing to normal, to your normal relaxed breath. Let your belly soften. You don't have to hold in your stomach. Allow your body to relax.

I want you to start relaxing your body, starting with your scalp, your forehead, the little muscles around your eyes, your jaw, your mouth. As you read this, you'll feel the areas of your body responding to the words and the energy on these pages. Notice how much tension you're releasing around your jaw and mouth. It might even be comfortable to let your mouth hang open. Release the tension around your ears, the sides of your head, your neck. Remember to breathe. Now you're going to release tension in your shoulders, arms, hands, chest, back, belly, and lower back. Now just let your hips go. Let your hips relax and breathe. Let your thighs get heavy, relax all the little muscles around your knees, your lower legs and feet. You're doing well.

Now you're going to give thanks to your Divine Creator; your highest and purest guides; angels; helpers; ascended masters; and your higher self, your authentic self. Imagine you have a tube of light coming down from the heavens, coming in through the top of your head. It's the brightest and purest light you've ever seen, and it's coming in through the top of your head, filling you up with that pure, white light, all the way through your body. It's filling up your head, torso, legs, arms; it's continuing down and out through the bottoms of your feet, down into the center of the Earth. This tube of light starts to encompass you. It's not just within you; it's all around you, as well. This tube is your connection to Spirit, and it's always accessible to you.

Now focus your attention on your feet. Imagine that you have tree roots or cables coming from the bottoms of your feet, down into the Earth, going down to the center of the planet. You're connected these grounding cables to the deepest part of the Earth. This helps you stay centered and grounded, even while deep healing is taking place. You're safe and Mother Earth has partnered with you in this lifetime, to help facilitate your healing.

When you feel complete, wiggle your fingers and toes and come back into the room. You'll take this relaxation, your connection with Source, and your connection with Mother Earth with you, throughout the day. If you ever feel disconnected from Source, your higher self, or the Earth, repeat this meditation as often as you like.

~ PART 2 ~

THE STAGES OF SOUL DEVELOPMENT

"... there is nothing in this life that happens 'to' you that is not actually 'for' you."

~ CHAPTER 3 ~

INFANT SOULS

NOW WE'RE ON TO OUR FIRST LEVEL OF SOULS! The first level of soul development includes the most grounded group of souls on the planet at this time, the infant souls. They are the newest souls to incarnate and they're here in the smallest numbers. At some point, we won't have any more of these baby souls here at all. They will all have graduated out of this phase into the later levels of development, because (as I understand it) there are no new human souls being created from Source at this time, as we are in the final stages of this creation cycle. Every new soul starts out at this level. As we are all headed toward higher levels of awareness and understanding, the older souls can help the younger souls forge ahead, like families do with siblings.

It's important to remember that even if you're an older soul, you will still have to deal with some infant soul issues. That's just part of the way we are built. We move on to higher levels while we still have yet to resolve some residue of the lower level issues. This is where the chakras come in. We hold those issues in our subtle bodies, in the chakra system. (Refer to the previous chapters for more details on this.) So, if you feel like an older soul, but you can relate to some of the conditions associated with the younger souls, that's completely normal. As an older soul, you'll just have more tools and access to higher levels of awareness to help you heal. Remember that it's not a race and efficiency isn't necessarily the goal. Learning how to move through your own development while not judging others or yourself is far more important than where you are in this process.

The level one souls are like the babies of the soul realm, exploring their world and learning how to survive physically, emotionally and spiritually. There is also a lot of energy focused on discovering how to live in peace with the Earth, other human beings and the spirit world. These souls have a special connection to the planet. They feel closer to Mother Earth and all that she has to offer than any other soul group does. Survival, social order, community, and personal security are the main areas of focus for these souls.

Social Order and Options

We spiritually look to the infant souls for a connection to our roots. Many of these souls live in tribal-type cultures in less developed countries. They tend to embrace the traditional culture that they were born into, as well as the individual role they have known since birth. An infant soul won't question why they are a hunter or why they have to help plow the fields, and these are typical jobs for these folks. They do the job they have always done, usually in the same way that their fathers, grandfathers, great-grandfathers, etc. have always done it.

These souls don't question their place on the planet. They know that they belong where they are. This can spark some jealousy from older souls, who have so many options that they don't ever really feel like they belong anywhere and tend to second guess and question every move they make. In most infant soul's lives, they're born with about six different options to choose from, whether they're in an actual indigenous tribe or a more modern group of some sort. The most common options are: hunter/provider, food preparer, healer/shaman, chief/leader, animal caretaker, or child/home caretaker. What a huge difference between the simplicity of the infant soul's options and the complex options of the other levels of soul development!

There are spiritual teachers, healers and leaders within every soul phase. The healer/shamans of the baby soul realm help the community understand the cycles of life, the relationship with the Earth, the traditions and the omens. They also are the metaphysicians of the group, sharing their healing knowledge from experience, but also from intuition. There are a multitude of practices associated with the term "shaman," but in general, a shaman acts as a mediator between the physical and the spirit world, and through that interaction, brings healing on every level. In our current era, there is a fascination among many older souls when it comes to shamanism. It's attractive to older souls because it speaks to our soul's history; we "remember" how it felt to be a younger soul and we can call on those ancient energies to help us heal. For all of us, at some point, in at least one of our lifetimes, we've either experienced healing from a shaman or we ourselves were the shaman.

Motivations, Survival, and Community

Infant souls are learning how to work together to survive and how to rely on each other and the planet to sustain them. They can't truly thrive until everyone learns how to work together, so there is a huge emphasis placed on the needs, health and safety of the group, rather than the needs of the individual. Part of the soul's growth for these young souls includes getting in touch with their own individual feelings, separate and unique from whatever group, family, tribe or community they find themselves in. That can be pretty frightening for them, because it's not going to be the popular way of perceiving their world. They can be considered selfish or rogue in their group, and many times are putting their lives at risk by speaking out about what they believe or how they feel.

Deep down they know that they could be shunned or shut out if they develop beyond the centralized group that they're involved with. You can imagine that—if you're in a tribal culture and you get kicked out of the tribe—it could be a life or death experience. It's an enormous risk and takes an extraordinary amount of bravery to grow beyond the infant soul way of thinking. To facilitate that growth, self-confidence becomes the most important quality we can have going for us, and self-doubt the biggest obstacle. It's our perceptions and the actions taken in those courageous moments that help us grow into the next level of our soul's development. We've all been there at one point, early in our soul's growth. In this lifetime, you might have experienced a situation when you've had to break free from a group, religion, workplace, family, or a marriage; you felt that your values and confidence had upgraded from where you began, and the result was a breakage in the relationship. You could have even felt like it was life or death to leave the situation. That's an indicator some unhealed infant soul issues.

If you've been through something like that in this life, then you can have a small glimpse into the life condition of an infant soul. But instead of having one situation that requires incredible bravery that you can heal from and move on, it's an everyday event for them. Instead of worrying about losing acceptance and love, these young souls are worried about actual survival and losing their lives. If you're thrown out of an earth-based culture and left all alone to fend for yourself, the chances of survival are dramatically decreased. Imagine how that must feel, and how the choice between remaining a conformist or thinking outside of the norm would feel like life or death. This is one of the biggest challenges for infant souls. Thankfully, we all eventually rise above our fear and doubt and move on to the next level.

Where on Earth Are the Baby Souls?

Although many of these souls live in less-developed areas, some can be found on the outskirts of cities, usually homesteading or living off the land. Those of us living in more modern, fast-paced societies can tend to either glamorize the basic-survival lifestyle of these level one souls, or judge them as unsophisticated and superstitious. As more and more older souls are craving simplicity in their lives, the glorification of younger soul's lifestyles will come up more and more. These young souls are learning about their relationship to the planet and to each other in a primal way, and that can feel nostalgic and enticing to older souls.

There are multiple levels within each soul level. So, while there are bright, positive examples of every soul type, there also can be a dark side to younger souls. They're still working out some of the basics of humanity. Very young infant souls can tend toward mental illness or criminal behavior if they are moved into busy cities or active modern societies. They are still learning right from wrong on a spiritual level, so if they do engage in criminal behavior, remorse and empathy are usually lacking.

The reason that this darker sub-group doesn't typically have empathy or compassion is because those are traits that are developed in the higher chakras. So until those chakras are more developed, empathy, unconditional love and compassion can be taught to some degree, but they won't be a natural outpouring of the first level infant soul.

Many of our world's psychopaths, sociopaths, and serial killers are infant souls; thankfully, these types represent only a tiny segment of the infant soul population. Not that someone of a different soul age couldn't commit a horrible crime; it just becomes more and more rare to have that type of activity, the older and more developed the soul becomes. To a point, unconditional love, compassion and empathy can be modeled for a baby soul that's become unbalanced, but those traits won't be natural hallmarks of this soul, once they've become that deeply unbalanced.

Taking Care

Infant souls are always longing for someone to take care of them. This doesn't stem from a "feeling" of powerlessness, but from of an actual inability to function in the modern world. So if you've ever thought to yourself,

"I wish someone would just take care of me," you're not a newborn soul, because such a soul wouldn't have the fleeting thought; they would just require the help. An older soul would have that feeling of wanting someone to take care of them when they have an emotional or physical wound that resulted in damage to the first chakra, the root chakra.

If this sounds like you, or if you've had trouble taking care of basic needs like survival, shelter, food, and establishing personal security, or have lots of group or family issues, then you have some root chakra wounding that will start to heal right now, as you're reading this. These wounds that originated during your incarnations as an infant soul (many lifetimes ago) show up in your current life so you can heal your soul, so you can continue your soul's development. We develop the root chakra from our in utero time until age 7, and then again between the ages of 50–56. If you think back to your life before you were 7 years old, that's when your root chakra wounding most likely surfaced.

These issues can take many forms: Maybe your parents were often worried about money and you took on those feelings. Or maybe you moved around often. If you had a parent in the military, it's would be very common for you to have root chakra issues because of your lack of emotional roots in a specific geographic area. Maybe you experienced childhood illnesses and had some physical survival issues, or your mother had a difficult labor. If you were adopted or not raised with your birth family, this can also contribute to root chakra issues. You'll find a more complete list of the ways these issues can manifest at the end of this chapter.

So you can now see that regardless of your soul's age, these issues exist for all of us to some degree. It's your soul's desire to be free from the fear and pain associated with old trauma, so congratulations on taking the step that you're taking right now to move forward. You didn't come across this book by accident; it's time to heal.

The Root

All of us are born with all of our chakras or energy centers in place. The chakras are natural vortices of energy that affect every aspect of our being—physical, emotional, and spiritual. While we heal, purify and work with every chakra in every lifetime, there are correlations between soul levels and intense chakra development.

As I mentioned, the energy center that is highlighted during this first soul growth phase is the root chakra. This chakra is the center for our survival issues, including food, shelter, the concept of being part of a village or community, and the more physical aspects of living on the planet. For the infant soul, the perceptions of self and of life flow through this chakra. While these souls spend most of their time and energy looking externally for answers and help, the inner resources of this chakra are firing on all cylinders to help them grow.

There's an additional sub-chakra that's at play here and bears mentioning. The earth star chakra is not contained within the *physical* body system; it's in the subtle body system. It's located about 12–18 inches below the bottoms of the feet. It's the connection between the subtle energy body and the energy of the planet. This chakra aligns our entire energetic system with the Earth's energy. It's the grounding point for every human being, and when it's balanced and harmonious, we feel deeply connected to our bodies, our energy system, and the Earth. We hold the karmic patterns from our previous lifetimes in this chakra, and it distributes the patterns throughout the chakra system whenever we're ready to heal ourselves. It also brings us the ability to feel steady and balanced, physically, emotionally and spiritually.

One of the many beautiful aspects of infant souls is that they are approaching life from the viewpoint of the earth star chakra, as well as the root chakra. The earth star perspective allows them to naturally feel connected to the Earth, the entire universe, and their own inner power. This is also the mechanism that pushes them to work toward a cause greater than themselves, whatever that cause may be; it's typically survival-based.

The root chakra, located at the base of the spine, holds the majority of the fear that we all experience on a regular basis, including feelings of belonging or the lack thereof. The level-one soul has so much energy in these two lower chakras (and not much refinement in the others) that they will tend to gravitate to the earth religions, mystical experiences, myths and legends, with an overarching, generally fear-based way of thinking, feeling and living. And for all of us, we can become overwhelmed with fear if the earth star and the root chakras aren't healthy, strong, and balanced, regardless of your soul's age. While these chakras are developing, fear seems to be the operational word of the day.

> The root chakra is the seat of our sense of survival and willingness to live. We develop this chakra during our infant soul lifetimes, and in this current lifetime, between the ages of 0 and 7 and again between the ages of 50 and 56. From this chakra, we learn how to take care of ourselves and protect and nourish ourselves. When this chakra is in need of repair, the issues of the infant-level soul present themselves, regardless of our soul's age. These issues can manifest as money issues, lower spinal issues, pervasive fear and anxiety, and doomsday thinking. Use the tools at the end of this chapter to begin healing those wounds.

When an infant soul is ready to move into the next phase of soul development, they've learned almost everything about how to protect themselves physically and live in harmony with the Earth, and these two lower chakras have helped them get there. When developed and in balance and harmony, both of these chakras can help us feel safe in the world and help us hone our instincts for self-protection and our ability to physically provide for ourselves. So certainly, infant souls can quickly move forward, embody more light, raise their frequency and enter the next phase, but—as with all types of growth—it can't be forced or taught with words. We're ready when we're ready.

Why would we put ourselves through all of this to grow and evolve our own souls? What's the point? It's interesting that the infant souls are (in a sense) closer to our Divine Source in terms of time, but the "forgetting process" that begins as soon as we incarnate into physical form means that we have no recollection of our deepest, most real connection—our connection with God or Source. Every lifetime that we experience brings us one step deeper into the "remembering process." Part of the journey includes getting back to a conscious connection and recollection of our Divine, true nature—as perfection, as part of the Divine Source, as being one with that God-spark. Our souls are all born from Divine Source; as soon as our soul is created, we forget that connection and, at the very same time, we begin our journey back to Source energy.

All along the way we get glimpses of our Divine connection, until we get to the old soul realm, where it's easily accessible and our natural way of being. If we're not in alignment with our spirit—our higher selves—we can look at younger souls with a feeling of judgment and can overlook what they bring to the planet. They bring a sense of wonder and mysticism, a feeling of connectedness with the Earth. If you're reading this and feel like you're older than an infant soul, remember that you had to experience this infant soul phase to get to where you are now. We don't get to skip stages of development. It's much like school: we have to begin with the basics and work our way up to the purer energies and practices.

~ ~ ~

Protection

Physical protection is a huge part of the infant soul's life. This means protection of self and protection of resources, money, food, family. In an ideal situation, we learn how to protect ourselves in this phase. When we have unresolved trauma from our time as infant souls, in this life we spiritually invite trauma to hit our lives in early childhood. This is always the way with our growth and healing. When something isn't healed from another time, it will continue to come up for us to address and resolve. Thankfully, we get multiple chances to resolve these issues.

If you tend to worry about someone breaking into your house, or being mugged or some other personal protection fear, that's an infant soul (and root chakra) issue coming up to be healed. See the end of this chapter for some tools to help you do just that.

Older souls can have issues with these lower chakras, for sure, because in every physical lifetime the chakras are present and are being honed and purified. The only reasons an older soul would have an issue with the lower chakras (meaning they were either born with that issue or something happened in this current lifetime that negatively impacted those chakras) would be because there is an aspect of that older soul that hasn't completely made peace with, forgiven themselves for, or integrated the aspects of the time when they were an infant soul themselves. If you're an old soul and you were born with or have root chakra issues, such as a spinal problem in your lower-back area, chronic bladder infections, or an intense fear of poverty, then you know there's still work to be done to make peace with your lives as an infant soul.

While physical needs and issues tend to take center stage with these youngest souls, they are also struggling with how they feel emotionally. "How do I feel?" is a difficult but prominent line of self-questioning during this level. Because of the earth star and root chakra entrainment with this phase, many times the answer to that question will be, "I feel like I need other people. I'm uncomfortable, and I need others, but it's only because I'm not yet capable of meeting my own needs as an individual." The feelings that are present are not usually deep emotions of belonging, but rather fear-based emotions centering on survival.

The survival fear that is always present in infant souls is not usually resolved within their earliest lifetimes, but rather when they've had enough incarnations to move into the second-level, the child-soul realm. Humans of every soul age have the instinct to survive; it just happens to be one of the overarching themes of this phase. The odds of an infant soul reading this book are slim to none; they are not typically interested in soul progression. It would feel overwhelming and even frightening to someone in that phase.

They don't have an inward compass that would help guide them to what's right and wrong; everything is about "me." This is not just focused on either physical or emotional or (even) spiritual needs; it's "all of the above." Inner emotional and psychological work isn't commonly present in infant souls because they're new to the planet. Since they've only had a minimal number of lifetimes, there hasn't yet been much growth beyond the goals of survival.

Cause and Effect

Have you ever experienced something in nature that was terrifying, like a hurricane, a tornado, a flood? We all have some fear around these events, whether or not we've actually been a victim of them in this lifetime. Now think of a tribe that lives off the land, has a tradition of connection with the Earth, and a fear of all that they cannot control: the weather, the seasons, invaders, intrusions. Myths and scary stories are passed down in these groups to try to explain why they're justified in their fear. The difference between a level-one soul's fear and a higher-level soul's fear is the idea of punishment.

If a snake bites an infant soul, instead of looking at the symbolism of the snake as older souls might (transformation, shedding your skin) or the more practical view (you shouldn't have walked where the snake was), it's typically seen as punishment. For that matter, most of the physical issues that infant souls deal with on a regular basis (like drought and famine) are all typically viewed as punishment.

It's easy to look at those who fall into this category and either judge them or glorify them for their simpler, primitive ways, but either way, you have been in that group at some point. You have successfully overcome the paralyzing fear of being a newborn soul, trying to make your way through tradition, starvation, and tremendous physical hardship.

How do you know if you're dealing with an infant soul? If the person is full of fear and has an inability to function in modern society, that's typical. As older souls, we have to remember that soul growth doesn't happen because someone tells us about it and/or we intellectually learn about it, and then we're able to jump to the next level. Soul growth happens through awareness and perception adjustments, which are specifically internal experiences that are prompted and encouraged by external experiences. So the trigger for growth for all souls will most likely be external or physical, but the growth happens internally. Awareness slowly increases. Perception gradually shifts. Light begins to be shed on new concepts and ideas.

This seems to me to be the slowest of all of the soul growth levels. Many people stay in the infant level for several lifetimes. Why? Because of their fear of moving forward, their fear of change. It doesn't make sense to the infant soul, even when they are intellectually very intelligent, for them to change, or grow, or listen to the inner voice that is tired of being scared.

They will gravitate toward a tribe that has a few older souls to hold things steady. Or they'll become the loner in the shack in the remote wilderness. (This is not to say that everyone who hermits away in the remote wilderness, Thoreau-style, is an infant soul. There are older soul ages that gravitate toward solitude as well.). The difference lies in the motivation for the isolation. Why is the person pulling back from society? Is it fear... or a desire for peace and calm? The younger soul will surely be motivated by fear.

When you encounter someone in this soul group, you

may notice their attachment to the Earth and the animal-pack quality of their thinking. The "pack" makes sense until it negatively impacts survival, just like being a loner makes sense until it's not possible. Emotional connection and feelings of loyalty, love, empathy and gratitude don't generally rise to the surface here. Gratitude for the Earth, yes, but also fear of punishment from that same nurturing Mother Earth.

And remember, too, that all of us develop neurologically and maturity-wise, as well.

Typically, we don't *really* settle into our current soul age and start to live accordingly until around age 40. At that point, we'll be able to access and use so much of the wisdom that we've gathered from our many lifetimes. Before that, we're still banging around like a person in the dark, not able to access where we really are, soul-wise.

Until that point, we're not usually able to relax into our true selves, and really use all of that hard-earned wisdom that we've gained from all of the other lifetimes. Some people hit that point a few years earlier or later, but typically we need about thirty-five to forty-five years to get there. So what if someone passes away before age thirty-five or forty? Typically, those people were in this lifetime to work on a specific issue from a previous incarnation. They were here to complete something, to finish out a cycle. When it's complete, they go ahead and regroup on the other side.

People in other soul levels can help infant souls develop and grow, by showing them the more balanced energy of the lower chakras. For example, someone who is not an infant soul can help solve a survival issue. Providing access to clean water, safe food supplies, sanitation, medical care—these are ways that older souls can help infant souls. These are not just kind, generous things to do; they actually positively influence the growth and evolution of those souls, by somewhat easing their physical burdens of survival, while they also model how well-developed lower chakras operate—a knowing that survival issues don't have to be enveloped in intense fear. There can be problem-solving that addresses a very real need in a logical, resourceful way, without resignation, desperation or panic. Lower chakra solutions to lower chakra issues.

Another way to help young souls is to project a broader understanding of the concept of the village. We don't have to look alike, sound alike, dress alike, want the same dinner, or speak the same language in order to help each other. These ideas are paramount for the infant soul to be exposed to as they progress into the next level, the child soul. Not every older soul has fully integrated these concepts either, but the majority of the paralyzing fear has to be vibrationally elevated, in order to "graduate" to the level of "child" soul, or level two. That's when the issues of being different and coping with fear and power become intensely real and potentially divisive in a more emotional way.

We also want to be mindful of trying to alter the way of life of infant souls too much. Helping to improve life conditions is admirable and will be received well, but taking the primitive infant soul out of their chosen area and forcing a modern, fast-paced, technology-heavy lifestyle will not yield a positive result with that soul. Their mind/body/soul/spirit complex cannot withstand those types of pressures, and this is where we have psychotic breaks, criminal activity, and fear-based issues that result in imprisonment or institutional confinement.

We cannot teach an infant soul to be intellectually and emotionally healed enough to allay the fear that they naturally hold. They haven't had enough upper chakra development for them to be well-adjusted in a modern, fast-paced lifestyle. For that matter, one could argue that none of us can easily be well-adjusted in the current modern life conditions, regardless of our soul level.

The overall growth of the infant soul will be focused on the issues of the earth star and root chakras, which include:

- The majority of energy being focused on basic survival
- Ancestral memories
- Tribal energy, with a deep need to belong
- "I'm safe as long as I'm with the group."
- Deep connection with Mother Earth and with their physical body
- Not comfortable in the modern world
- Outstanding courage and resourcefulness
- Very strong will to live
- Karmic patterns and generational ties

~ ~ ~

Healing and Progress

All souls are progressing through these growth stages more rapidly than ever before because of the increase in the Earth's frequency. When we alleviate some of the survival issues associated with young souls, we help them develop into the next level, and we help ourselves move forward from wherever we are in our own soul's development by healing our own issues from that phase.

Here's what you can do:

- Bring clean water to areas that don't have it
- Bring food to those who are in need, locally or globally
- Contribute to disaster relief efforts, either with time, prayer, goods or money
- Contribute to education locally and in developing countries
- Give your unwanted clothing to those who need it
- Contribute to housing issues
- Honor tribal culture by purchasing Fair Trade items that are made by artisans in developing countries

Another great way to heal your own root chakra issues is to freely and lovingly give either money, prayers, time or gifts. This is the opposite of worrying about not having enough, which is the main symptom of survival issues. This is why tithing or giving to spirituality-based causes is so healing. We use the survival issue (root chakra) to connect with spiritual nourishment (crown chakra) and in doing so, we align all of the chakras beautifully.

How do you know if you have unhealed issues from when you were an infant soul?

- If you have money issues that you'd like to improve
- If you have issues with dizziness or vertigo
- If you have problems with your sacrum or lowest vertebrae
- If you have chronic bladder infections or other issues in this area
- If you regularly find yourself hiding away, not wanting to interact with others
- If you carry fear of being kicked out of your family or group
- If you need a firm role in the family or your work, and have trouble making adjustments
- If you find yourself worrying about survival or survival-based issues regularly
- If you are waiting for an economic crash, food shortage, water shortage, natural disaster, or some other doomsday event

"Soul age is not an indicator of superiority or inferiority. It's a gauge for compassionate understanding of ourselves and others."

You can use these tools here to help you heal and move forward!

Affirmations

I trust the flow of life.

I trust in the power of life.

I trust the process of life.

I feel at home in my body.

I'm sustained and nourished by nature.

Centering

Imagine you have tree roots or strong cables coming from the base of your spine and the bottoms of your feet, extending down into the center of the Earth. These grounding roots or cables are helping you to stay focused and grounded while you are recalibrating and healing the issues of the root chakra, using the techniques and meditation below.

Mantra

Lam (sounds like Lahm, elongating the LAAA sound gently into the AHMM)

This is the sound that helps to balance the root, and repetition of this sound, while holding the hand mudra described below, will give you a quick balancing, anytime you feel fearful or anxious.

Mudra

Chin Mudra/Jnana Mudra

Benefits: Helps spiritual awakening, reduces depression, helps with focus during meditation.

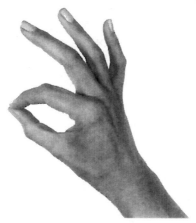

Chin Mudra/Jnana Mudra

Technique: Sit in a comfortable position, and touch your index finger to your thumb, on each hand. Hold for 5 to 60 minutes, incorporating a mantra or an affirmation from this chapter if you like. Two options (experiment with both options if this is a new mudra for you):

1. With your hands resting on your thighs or knees, if your hands are resting palms down, the mudra facilitates a feeling of emotional and physical groundedness, connected with the root chakra.

2. If the palms are facing up, the mudra facilitates feelings of openness in the crown chakra, with a lightness of spirit.

Guided Meditation to Heal and Purify the Root Chakra

Take a few deep breaths and allow yourself to relax. Exhale any tension, and let your breathing fall into a nice, relaxed rhythm. Let your belly soften. You don't have to hold in your stomach. Let your whole midsection relax.

Pay attention to any tension in your body and begin releasing it, into relaxation. Just reading these words will help your body and mind begin to gently release. Notice and relax your scalp, your forehead, the little muscles around your eyes, your jaw, your mouth. Release the tension around your ears, the sides of your head, your neck. Remember to breathe. Now release tension in your shoulders, arms, hands, chest, back, belly, lower back. Now let your hips relax and breathe. Let your thighs get heavy, relax the little muscles around your knees, your lower legs, and feet.

Now you're going to give thanks to the Great Spirit; your highest and purest guides; angels; helpers; ascended masters; and your higher self, your authentic self. Imagine you have a tube of light coming from the heavens, coming in through the top of your head. It's the brightest and purest light you've ever seen, and it's filling you up with that pure white light, all through your body. It's filling up your torso, legs, and arms. It's continuing down through the bottoms of your feet, down into the center of the Earth. This tube of light starts to encompass you. It's not just within you; it's all around you as well.

Now you're going to bring in the energy that your root chakra (at the base of your spine) needs at this moment.

This is red energy. You're bringing in the energy of the sacred red rocks of Sedona, Arizona. You're bringing in the energy of the red clay of the Earth. This is the red of the dawn, the red of the sunset. Breathe in that energy. Imagine that color coming up from the center of the Earth and from the environment around you, collecting at the base of your spine, where that root chakra is. Your root chakra is bringing in the energy that's natural to it, that red energy of the Earth. Imagine that red energy is swirling at the base of your spine. It's building and swirling, and you can know that exactly what needs to happen with that energy, is now happening.

You can let your mind relax. You can either hold these images in your mind now, or you can just read these words and relax. If you have intrusive thoughts, they're not actually intrusive; they're just fine. There's no need to judge them; you can just let them go. Just be here now. Just by reading these words, healing is beginning.

Now you're going to address the things that you've stored in that chakra, the root chakra. We're addressing the things that you've stored in your subtle body through ancestral patterns, lineage issues, past lifetimes, and this lifetime. You've needed everything that you've stored in this chakra until this point in time. Now you'll choose more consciously what you need and what you don't. Everything you've stored in this chakra has also affected your cells, your organs, your systems, and your thinking. It's affected you physically, mentally, emotionally, spiritually, and now here you are, making conscious choices about what you want to include. So you're going to give thanks for all of the wisdom, love, and everything you've gotten either from this lifetime, other lifetimes, from your ancestors, or from your lineage. You're going to give thanks for everything you've learned from the challenging aspects, the things that weren't so happy, and the things that were very happy.

You're giving thanks for all of the wonderful things that have been working within you, like the will to survive, the ability to survive, decisiveness when it's needed, taking action, being able and willing to travel to the far and unknown with bravery, courage, and resourcefulness. As you're giving thanks to these energies, you're bringing them in, you're amplifying them. The energies of positive innocence, positive vulnerability, spontaneity, the energies of vitality, joy, and living. The sense of belonging. Feelings of connection with other human beings, the feeling of joy and life, endurance, your connection to nature, flowing with the rhythm of life, the ability to flow with the seasons. You're giving thanks to all of this in all aspects of time and space, in all aspects of you—physical, emotional, mental, ethereal, astral—in every possible way, including aspects that are known to you, and aspects that are unknown.

Now you're going to give thanks for, and you're going to release any and all of the following that you are no longer working with, that you no longer need, either from this lifetime or past lifetimes, or from ancestral and lineage issues. You are now releasing any and all unwillingness to live, all fear, all feelings of lack of control. You're releasing egoism and narcissism. You're releasing compulsiveness and greed. You're neutralizing and releasing all of these: guilt, uncontrolled drives, lack of trust, disorientation. You're giving thanks for the experience, but at the same time you are continuing to neutralize, release and give thanks for any times when you've experienced addiction or mental weakness, a lack of belonging, a lack of connection, or a lack of loyalty. You're neutralizing and giving thanks for all of the lessons and everything that you've learned, all of the wisdom, and all of the love.

And now, you'll complete the releasing of any of these energies that you are no longer using, and any others that I did not mention that are not in your highest good, that are no longer serving you. In a moment, I want you to count down from ten to one, and you will release what you no longer need, whatever is no longer contributing to your highest benefit, and no longer helping you achieve your highest good and your purest joy.

As you count down from ten to one, you'll neutralize and release all of that. Ten, nine, eight, seven, six, five, four, three, two, one. Take a deep breath, and now exhale big, and release it. Perfect.

You may feel hot, tired, or emotional. You may feel a hot flash, but this is not your hormones! If you feel emotional, that's okay. Just let it keep flowing through. You're only releasing what your higher self has agreed to release, whatever you are done with. Keep breathing. Imagine that you have deep roots coming from the base of your spine, and the bottoms of your feet that go all the way down into the core of the Earth. These deep roots can be like tree roots; they can be like cables. Whatever they are, they're keeping you grounded and centered, reminding you of your sense of safety, your sense of security. That is real. You are safe. All is well.

You're now going to create healing from all of your lifetimes as a first level infant soul and as a child in this lifetime. Affirm: "I allow all appropriate, optimal, beneficial, and benevolent healing from all of my lifetimes as a first level infant soul, and for this lifetime, from the day, the hour, the minute, and the second of my physical birth on this planet, up through the very last moment of age seven. From the moment I was born until my last day, my last moment of being age seven, I allow all of the appropriate, optimal, beneficial, and benevolent healing."

This is when you were learning how to build trust. You were building trust with your environment, with your family, your culture, and ultimately with yourself. What a huge responsibility for a little one to learn how to build that trust! Every person, every situation, every environment, culture, everything that you encountered from the moment of your birth until that last moment of age seven was on purpose, to help you learn how to build trust within yourself at some point, and that point might be today. It might not have been back then. It might be tomorrow, it might be next year, but without a doubt, the groundwork was laid in perfect form, even if it didn't seem perfect at the time.

All of the frequencies in your body are being harmonized right now. They're being optimized. Your glands, your organs, your systems, your blood, all of the water in your body—they are all being upgraded and optimized as you read this. As we close this healing meditation, give thanks for the awareness of your own body, and embrace the optimal will to live, to fully live.

Breathe in that will to live. Breathe deeply into the will to live, the life that you were meant to live with joy, peace, safety, and stability, and more. Now just keep breathing. Be present in your body. Just rest and relax.

You have a fully awakened, beautifully balanced, root chakra. All of your other chakras are starting their realignment and recalibration process in preparation for the healing that will come in the following chapters. Repeat this process as often as you like.

For a free recording of this meditation and other audios that you can listen to and follow along with, visit our special webpage for readers of this book: alyssamalehorn.com/ hoiys

~ CHAPTER 4 ~

CHILD SOULS

"Our deepest fear is not that we are inadequate. Our deepest fear is that we are powerful beyond measure. It is our light, not our darkness that most frightens us. We ask ourselves, 'Who am I to be brilliant, gorgeous, talented, fabulous?' Actually, who are you not to be? You are a child of God. Your playing small does not serve the world."
~ Marianne Williamson, *A Return to Love*

ONCE WE HAVE INCARNATED TEN TO THIRTY TIMES or so, and have moved through all of the phases of life as an infant soul, we begin the child soul phase, where we start to have more of an impact on our society. This adjustment brings us out of our focus on the physical world, and into more of our emotional life. Right now, child souls are a little bit more plentiful on the planet than infant souls are. They're still not in the majority, but a there are a few more of them than the infant souls.

And again, remember that the purposes of this book are to allow you to drop any judgment you might have about anyone who is different than you are or who thinks differently, and to heal any unresolved issues from when you were a younger soul, so you can move forward into your naturally progressed state of enlightenment. It's not just psychological; it's not just emotional, mental, or physical. It's what you are able to understand on a soul level. All of this works together. Another reminder: as you're reading this, you're receiving healing transmissions of energy that will help you integrate these concepts on every level.

Depending on our soul's age, we tend to gravitate toward different types of environments. Just as an infant soul will choose to incarnate in a more remote area and in some sort of tribal aspect of community, a child soul will tend to incarnate in a more conservative environment or in an environment where organized religion is prevalent, where there is conformity. Conformity equals safety to a child soul.

Child souls contribute a good sense of order on the planet and they enjoy regimented groups. This can lead to being somewhat rigid and conservative in their thinking. They prefer having structure, a firm schedule, and knowing what comes next. You'll see many child souls go into military service, law enforcement, and other conformist environments with a culture of rules. Of course, there are other soul ages that can be drawn to military service or law enforcement, but it's common for child souls. Hopefully it's becoming clear that—at this time in our collective evolution—we need every soul type on the planet, in order for us to have balance.

A large part of the child soul's journey involves feeling left out and not knowing where they belong. If you're an older soul and identifying with these feelings, that's very common. It's one of the commonalities between these two soul ages, level two (child) and level five (old). In our physical lives, you'll notice that children and elderly folks seem to have some traits in common, as well. This is a similar situation, and both of these soul groups can tend to have some unlikely similarities, even if they don't fully understand each other.

Child souls are usually unaccepting of souls that are older than they are and souls younger than they are. They tend to get angry and even disparaging of older souls; they perceive them as weak and without proper control. This is because the older soul is focused on personal, inner freedom and the child soul is focused on regimentation and control. You can see how the differences of perception can be divisive. These are a few of the more challenging characteristics of the child soul: the lack of understanding and lack of acceptance of people that are in different soul phases.

It's difficult for a child soul to see gray areas; to them, everything is black and white, or "us" and "them." When you're a child soul, there can be a real distrust of people who are different. When a child soul is in the early development of this second level, there will be no convincing them that those who look different than they do or think differently than they do could possibly be acceptable. If you see yourself in this aspect of the child soul description, then part of your job is to stretch yourself to be able to see more gray areas, and to understand that people who are different from you aren't necessarily wrong or defective in some way.

Older souls will typically go through a similar phase.

However, in the older soul, it's a short-lived phase and can be adjusted through healing the emotional wounds of our childhood in this lifetime. These wounds originate in trauma during the child soul level in previous lifetimes and present themselves in the sacral chakra, located just below the navel. Knowing this can help you realize that there's nothing wrong with you if you feel that way, and that you will eventually shift into a belief that perhaps you could trust people who are different or believe differently than you do.

The sacral chakra is the seat of our sense of feeling and intimacy. We develop this chakra during our child-soul lifetimes, and in this current lifetime between the ages of 8 and 14, and again between the ages of 57 and 63. We learn how to experience pleasure in this chakra and how to feel safe even when we're relaxing. When this chakra is in need of repair, the issues of the child level soul present themselves, regardless of our soul's age. These issues can look like intimacy problems, trust issues, belonging issues, sexual dysfunction, and a fear that relaxing will be considered negligent. "If I relax, I'm dropping the ball." Use the tools at the end of this chapter to begin healing those wounds.

As the soul grows and develops, the difference between the infant-soul level and the child-soul level regarding the energy of belonging becomes more apparent. The infant

soul *has* to belong to survive. The child soul just wants
to and there's some new emotional energy in it. We still
see a lot of fear in this level, but the fear isn't just directed
toward external, uncontrollable circumstances or strictly
survival issues. This new fear now stems from an inner
feeling of lack, specifically lack of connection and lack of
feeling understood. It's true that in every soul level, we
can experience these types of feelings, but in the second-
level soul, those feelings are the driving force behind most
decisions and actions.

This level is where we learn right from wrong. The
learning of right from wrong doesn't mean that the child
soul will always want to do the right thing; there's some
experimenting here. As you can see, the child soul has
a lot in common with an actual child, even in physical
adulthood. It's highly unlikely that a child level soul will be
reading this, but should that occur, the energy transmitted
from these pages will help you move into the next level to
allow more acceptance into your life.

The child soul is looking out for themselves in a
different way. They're not just concerned with their
physical safety and wellbeing; they really want to feel good.
This is where they learn what feels good and what doesn't,
and where they learn how to manipulate the people around
them to get what they want. This becomes more complex
when they start to realize that they have a lot to offer, but
fears of not belonging or not being worthy underlie all of
the child soul's offerings. The manipulation of people, and
the manipulation of the physical environment and the inner
environment is how the child soul struggles to alleviate the
ever-present fear within them.

Control surges to the forefront in this level. Just like a young child says, "No! I can do it myself!" but then requires some assistance and begrudgingly accepts it, the child soul wants to feel completely self-reliant but still needs lots of help from souls with more experience. If you have serious trouble asking for and receiving help, you can be sure that you have some unhealed issues from when you were a child soul, which can then begin again in this lifetime between the ages of 8 and 14 and again between 57 and 63. It's common for older souls to carry these wounds. At the end of this chapter, you'll see some exercises to help you heal and release control issues, which are just cloaked versions of fear.

Child level souls will prefer strict, organized religion. Evangelical, fear-mongering, "fire and brimstone" preachers fall into this category. You might recall from the previous chapter that we have spiritual teachers in every level of soul development. The spiritual teachers and preachers of the child-soul realm tend to promise peace and redemption through the energy of fear, control and reminding their flock of their unworthiness. This is part of the need for a regimented lifestyle that is full of rules and authority, and also a part of the "us and them" mentality that's ever-present with child souls. It can feel very threatening to a child soul to see anyone who is not following the rules, especially their rules.

As I mentioned before, many military personnel and police are in this soul level. Not everyone who joins these organizations are child souls, but the child soul doesn't just enjoy the regimentation of these groups; they need it to feel stable and safe. They also require authority figures in their lives, so they have someone to energetically push up against, to help them grow. There are always some older souls mixed into the military and our police forces, but the majority of those attracted to these fields (if they stay in it and truly enjoy it) are in some stage of the child soul level. Those who enter these organizations and decide to pursue other paths after a relatively short time, are folks who have significant wounding from other lifetimes when they were a child soul. The re-immersion into that type of environment can be very healing, and when that healing is complete, they no longer need that type of structure.

As long as there are young souls on this planet, we need military and police. At this time, we have a pretty small number of child souls on Earth. The percentage of child souls is dropping steadily as we all embody more light and adjust our perceptions accordingly, along with our frequencies. Some countries have a higher population of child souls than others, as you may have gathered. Countries like China and areas like the Middle East have a high percentage of child souls, while the number of child souls is still pretty low in the U.S., not in the majority. As I mentioned, these numbers are dropping, as we all embody more light and develop ourselves soul-wise.

You can see how every phase is important, as long as we all are in the mix together. As everyone's individual light quotient rises and the collective frequency rises because of those individual light quotients, we will have less and less of a need for any military at all. We only require a military in the U.S. and other similar countries because there are so many young souls on the planet right now. Young souls are battling other young souls for control and "rightness."

Once our collective light quotient has moved fully into the other soul ages, the need for attacking and defending will subside. There is truly hope for peace, but it will take many more lifetimes before it's the norm on this planet.

If you're an older soul, there is no need to try to convince a child soul to express themselves in a different way than they naturally do. You can't push someone out of where they are, soul development-wise, and expect a different behavior. You can't "convince" an eight-year-old to do college level work, and the eight-year-old isn't being defiant or rebellious by not being able to do it. The same applies to soul ages and soul experience. We cannot control other people, nor would we want to. The higher level truth of what we really want is for everyone to express themselves and experience their lives exactly the way they are entitled to, exactly the way that they chose to, through the experiences that will best help them develop. If you're feeling some control issues and it's hard to connect with that higher truth, using the tools at the end of this chapter will help you resolve that pattern.

This also leads us to how important it is to leave judgment and criticism behind and actively send love and light to all souls in every stage of development. If we only honor and send love to souls in our own soul-age group (people whom we easily understand), we're not helping the younger souls to grow beyond their set point. As an added bonus, when we work on healing ourselves, we also transmit healing energy to others. Remember that if you're not a child soul now, you were at some point.

> "If you judge people, you have no time to love them." ~ Mother Teresa

Mantra Exercise

A mantra is a word or phrase that you repeat to yourself again and again, to shift your consciousness and transmit a specific energy into the world. You can use any word or phrase as a mantra, just make sure it represents a quality that you're wanting to embody and that it's framed in a positive way.

Mantra: Lokah samastah sukhino bhavantu (with emphasis on the first syllable of each word)

Translation: May all beings everywhere be happy and free, and may the thoughts, words, and actions of my own life contribute in some way to that happiness and to that freedom for all.

lokah: location, realm, all universes existing now

samastah: all beings sharing that same location

sukhino: centered in happiness and joy, free from suffering

bhav: the divine mood or state of unified existence

antu: may it be so; it must be so (transforms this mantra into a declaration)

For a free recording of this mantra and other audios that you can listen to and gain the benefits from, even while you sleep, visit our special webpage for readers of this book: alyssamalehorn.com/hoiys

Routine and Belonging

Just as a young child will feel safer, be better behaved, sleep and eat better when they are in a regimented routine, so the child soul needs routine to be able to live without chaos in their lives. Most of us really like having a routine, as it does help us all feel stable and secure in a world that doesn't offer much security. The difference is that the child soul feels out of control and very scared when the routine changes or requires adjustment. You may know someone who seems like an older soul, but has some of these issues with routine and needing to be right all the time. Healing the sacral chakra will help tremendously with those issues.

Child souls are wanting to belong so much, and are developing the part of themselves that can feel connected with other people in an emotional way, not just the physical survival connection of the infant soul. This is an incredible gift, because they will stop at nothing to meet the objectives of the overall group. The challenge comes when they adjust their beliefs to match the beliefs of the group to which they want to belong. Sometimes the adjustment isn't a positive one, and they can edge other people out who don't believe the same way they do, or the same way the group believes.

We see this pattern in cults and other organizations that demand that their members cut off communication and relationships with anyone outside of their group. A child soul can feel very special and feel like they finally belong somewhere when the group is exclusive in that way. If someone is an older soul and they find themselves in a group with those limitations, eventually they will outgrow the group as their sacral chakra issues begin to heal. The challenge is that healing can be very slow and painful in this situation, with feelings of isolation and desperation that must be moved through before true healing can occur.

The same dynamic can be seen in love relationships, where one or both of the people are in this soul level. The younger soul in the partnership can be manipulative and coerce the other person (of an older soul age) to cut off relationships outside of that primary relationship with them. The younger soul does this through making the older soul feel special and loved, but it's a control-based love. The younger soul can seem totally "head over heels," but the reality is that they are deeply afraid of being left behind or abandoned. The fear motivates them to exercise control over another person, under the guise of "love."

If you're an older soul, and find yourself in a relationship like this, you can know that you have some unhealed wounds that the younger soul is pointing out to you. It can seem strange to thank someone for triggering you, but that's the appropriate response. As an older soul, you will struggle for a while to remain autonomous or to break free from the control of the younger soul, and exhaust yourself in the process. Then you can thank the younger soul for waking up the part of you that still holds the fear of not belonging, or the part of you that was feeling neglected. The exercises at the end of this chapter will help provide clarity and movement forward where it's needed.

Crisis

One of the beautiful aspects of child souls is the ability to come together in a crisis. They can organize and mobilize like no other soul group, and the bravery of the child soul is awe-inspiring when they are in the middle to late stages of that phase. It's inevitable to see this courage in action after a disaster or some event that requires crisis management and group efforts. These souls can spring into action at a moment's notice when called to be a part of a group effort, especially where they're helping others. They love to be the helpers and the rescuers, not only for the admiration, but because they are genuinely good at caring for people and working in high-stress situations.

The challenge here is that, depending on where they are in their soul development, the innate ability to organize and mobilize can be used for good or for darkness. If they are in the late stages of the child soul phase, their skills are almost always used for a positive cause to help others, be it people they know, total strangers, animals or the environment. When they're good, they're really good!

However, if they are in the early stages of child soul development, then a soul of this age can be convinced that a group of people with a different viewpoint or religion or lifestyle is evil and should be punished, or (in a worst-case scenario) even destroyed. This is the energy that Hitler preyed upon in Nazi Germany. He invoked the child souls who wanted and needed desperately to belong.

It was the illusions of sameness and differentness that were the soul-level backbone of his plans. We know that anyone who believes that they are the only real purveyor of the truth (whatever they claim that truth to be) is a young soul. The beautiful diversity among humans can become terrifying representations of their own feelings of unworthiness and lack of belonging.

In the mind of the early stage child soul, "different" becomes defined as "bad, evil, less worthy," or (in the most extreme cases) "not permitted to occupy a place on the planet". Throughout the ages, these souls were the perpetrators of slavery as well. It's true that young souls are the only beings who could enslave other human beings and be completely and thoroughly convinced that there is nothing wrong with doing so. As a generality, those who were enslaved were older souls than their captors. This is also true for other tragedies like the Holocaust, where the victims were older souls than the military.

In my professional practice over the years, I've connected with countless client's relatives and friends in the spirit world. In some cases, I've connected with their departed loved ones who were victims of these atrocities, as well as those who perpetrated these crimes. While everyone in the spirit world has their own soul lessons that they're learning and their own specific reasons for agreeing to be involved in such darkness, there is a commonality that I've seen every time. Here it is: on the other side, the perpetrators have a much more difficult time and have spiritually made more sacrifices than the victims. I'm sure that can sound strange or unbelievable when you consider the pain and sacrifices made by the victims when they're here on Earth, but the perpetrators have agreed to feel totally disconnected from Divine Source energy (God or light) to learn the lessons that their soul needed to grow, to learn the early stages of empathy, and move forward. They abandon themselves and God. It's the ultimate self- and soul-betrayal.

The victims typically share with me that they initially felt abandoned by God, but then, after some time, they reconnected with Divine Source energy and after that they never felt alone again. This is another "symptom" of being an older soul: falling away from your true nature for the soul-level experience, and then reconnecting with that true nature, often all within the same lifetime. We'll get to more about old souls in Chapter 7.

In that life-between-lives time, when we're making our plans for our upcoming incarnation, why would an older soul agree to be a victim or enslaved by anyone at all, in any lifetime? There are three general reasons that are always involved in that decision, with innumerable specific reasons that are as unique as each person on the planet.

The first general reason is for the goal of understanding personal power and learning how to become empowered, through the contrasting experience of a perceived loss of power, the illusion of overall powerlessness, or self-abandonment (giving up). The bottom line that always comes out of these situations is that our self-imposed mental enslavement (our belief that we are powerless or our belief that we are not free) is initially extremely detrimental. However, it eventually becomes a far greater learning tool for us than any enslavement could be that comes from an outside source or is externally imposed.

The second reason includes the decision to play the role of victim in this life, because in other incarnations, the older soul has played the role of perpetrator. We all deeply want to understand our effect on others, and it's a natural, normal part of our growth process to empathize in a deep way. There's no better way to emotionally put yourself in someone else's shoes than to actually—physically—put yourself in their position. There is so much to be learned from every aspect of every situation, and older souls aren't happy unless they're learning and moving forward as efficiently as possible.

The third reason is to help the younger souls play out their curriculum, so they can experience the dramatic self-betrayal that is the crux of the misuse of power. We agree to help younger souls when we're in the spirit world, making our plans for our lives. We don't ever agree to help others without knowing that we will also be learning and gathering exactly what we need. What helps others learn and grow, helps us learn and grow. It's *always* a two-way street, beneficial for everyone, every time, without exception.

Smaller scale versions of this young soul scenario are also accurate, such as a husband who controls every move his wife makes. When seen from the outside, it may look like he holds militant strength in their home. In all of these examples, large and small, we know that an intense fear within the perpetrator is what is behind all of it. There's not really a graceful way to say that child souls have a very deep need to be seen as right. And if they change their minds, they were right then and they're right now. At this point in history, it's not as common on the planet for child souls to try to eradicate those who they perceive to be a threat to the way they believe, but unfortunately, in some parts of the world, it still is happening. Fortunately, most child souls are moving in the direction of helping others.

If you're an older soul and you become aware of these types of injustices, it's important to take whatever action you can, to help alleviate the suffering. Getting involved on any level will help you fulfill your own soul's mission, and at the same time will help the younger souls begin to see the light of their own Divinity. How to help? Focusing on sending prayer and energy, and actions such as giving time, resources, and money all help to bring more light and soul development to any situation that isn't in alignment with the God-spark within us. The good news is that as humankind continues to graduate to higher and higher levels of consciousness, there will be fewer and fewer of these atrocities.

History Repeating Itself

There have been young souls on the planet since the beginning of time, and every era has its history of control, war and human rights violations. If you're an older soul, you can be pretty sure that you participated in some of these issues when you were spiritually younger. Souls in the child phase will inevitably struggle with these power and authority crises.

Any control issues, large or small, that you have right now (in this lifetime) stem from when you were a young soul and either abused power or had no power. Those wounds were then brought to your attention when you were between the ages of eight and fourteen. You may have felt as though you had no power or didn't belong in your family or culture. It might have played out in a phase where you had no self-control. If unhealed, these issues can continue to plague you throughout your life. You might even think that it's a personality issue or just a character defect. You'll see improvement in your control issues if you take the steps at the end of this chapter to help heal those old wounds. Nothing feels better than freedom from our own self-imposed mental enslavement!

Right and Wrong

After leaving the infant soul level, because of its process of learning about the differences between right and wrong the child soul feels like it's very important to be on the "right" side of all issues. This is one of the reasons that they are drawn to strict religions that claim to be the sole keeper of the truth. The stricter the religion, the more child souls will be there. Many religions have a flexibility and understanding of human nature within them, but in the case of young souls, they can take any religion and see a starkly black and white view of the world. This can result in a self-serving, manipulated, or literal interpretation of religious texts such as the Bible or the Koran.

There is no arguing with the child soul about religious beliefs, so if you believe differently than they do, don't waste your time trying to open their minds to a different viewpoint. If they are identifying with a religious group, they "know" beyond a shadow of a doubt that they are on the side of what is good and what is right, and everyone else must be misguided, weak-minded, or even under evil influences.

When a level two soul falls short of the mark and does something that appears to be a fall from grace (like we've seen in the news in the past, e.g. an evangelical pastor engaging in drugs or soliciting prostitutes), then there is always a perceived "enemy" that can bear the brunt of the blame. "The devil made me do it" or some other terrible circumstance is usually to blame. While addiction is a very real disease, and most people who are in recovery from addiction can see their situation clearly, younger souls can use their addiction as the "enemy" that caused them to do something that hurt themselves or those they love. In those cases, the addiction is seen as something outside of themselves that is beyond their grasp. Taking responsibility and seeing the deeper reasons for our behavior can be very challenging for all of us at any soul age, but is especially difficult for these young souls.

If you're struggling with addiction, regardless of your soul's age, it's important to remember that you chose that life pattern when you were in the spirit world, before you incarnated. You chose it because you believed that you could most efficiently learn what your soul needed to learn from the viewpoint of an addict. It's not an affliction soul-wise, although it is a disease. You haven't been singled out and victimized by this genetic ailment. You're a brave soul who knew that you could be super-efficient in your soul's growth by venturing into those realms.

You knew that to get to the goal of self-love, it was going to take some time experiencing the opposite: self-abuse.

Choosing the journey of addiction in this lifetime isn't for the faint of heart, to be sure. But each person who has chosen that path knows that, through the lens of that hardship, they will eventually be able to see the Divine within themselves and others, and move into true freedom.

I believe that this is a difficult stage in soul development. When you're in it, you feel like you must "tow the line" and "color within the lines" all of the time, and God forbid you make a mistake! The ability to forgive ourselves and others when we're in these stages is extremely difficult. It's like breaking out of a concrete shell. You're holding on to guilt and shame for your own actions, while at the same time you are still blaming other people, addiction, illness, situations, or the devil for your actions. What an emotionally miserable, isolated, unstable place that can be! If every child soul would take a deep breath and say, "I forgive myself for being human," that alone would cause an interesting shift! If you're noticing that you have some unhealed issues from this phase, try saying that affirmation, as well. When we repeat affirmations over time, we allow the higher level truth to sink in and become part of us.

It's easy to love a child soul, just like it's easy to love actual children. They are confident (sometimes to a point of being arrogant), but they will defend you to the ends of the Earth (provided they believe the same way you do!) If this resonates with you, just know that your fear of being seen as wrong or feeling like you must step out on a limb to support what your society or group believes is right will subside more and more as time passes and you allow your frequency to rise naturally. You are learning how to use your wonderful ways of being, for the utmost betterment of yourself and the world.

The overall growth of the child soul will be focused on the issues of the sacral and the root chakras, which include:

- Lots of passion for being seen as right
- Addictions to lower-frequency triggers: 24-hour news channels, crime shows, gossip, judging others or self, fire and brimstone religion, physical and emotional toxins, scary movies
- Wants to help others and be the rescuer
- "I'm going to get them before they get me."
- "Retaliation is more honorable than forgiveness."
- Reproduction, in terms of having babies, but also reproducing other people's ideas; it's not really easy to check in and make a decision based on a new feeling
- Easier to make decisions based on unresolved fear or feeling victimized, rather than what would be the best for themselves or others
- Support of a group mentality
- "What's best for the group must be best for me."
- Needs rigid structure to be happy
- Working on decreasing judgment of others and allowing openness and acceptance to flourish

The best action to take to heal these issues within yourself is to include people in your life. The opposite energy is exclusion, so we want to bring in the higher vibration of inclusion. Worry less about whether or not you feel like you belong; just allow people to feel a sense of belonging with you. The best way to do this is to work on releasing judgment of others and yourself.

How do you know if you have unhealed issues from when you were a child soul that resulted in issues that arose in this lifetime between the ages of 8 and 14?

- If you have control issues that you'd like to shift
- If you regularly find yourself judging yourself and others negatively
- If being right is more important to you than having peace of mind
- If you constantly seek groups to validate your experience
- If you find yourself looking for low frequency distraction, like 24-hour news channels or some other fear-based entertainment
- If you feel disconnected from your feelings
- If you feel a fear of losing control
- If you feel disconnected from your body
- If you are uncomfortable with your sexuality
- If you overindulge in sexuality in any way, through thought or action
- If you carry the energy of shame around your body
- If you've experienced sexual abuse

Here are your sacral chakra tools to help you heal and move forward!

Affirmations

I am always in the right place at the right time.

I enjoy life with all of my senses.

I allow my natural creativity and joy to flow freely.

I lovingly accept my body and my sensuality.

Centering

Close your eyes and imagine a beautiful, natural pool with a waterfall. The water's crystal clear. You're approaching it, and you sense the power of the water. You step into the water and start swimming toward the waterfall. You can feel the mist. As you swim closer, your entire body feels the cleansing, creative, passionate energy of the waterfall. Stay in this space, sensing the energy of the water as long as you like.

(Anytime you feel creatively blocked, use your imagination and return to this lovely setting.)

Mantra

Vam (sounds like Vahm, elongating the VAAA sound gently into the AHMM)
    and
Lokah Samastah Sukhino Bhavantu

For a free recording of these mantras and other audios that you can listen to and gain the benefits from, even while you sleep, visit our special webpage for readers of this book: alyssamalehorn.com/hoiys

Mudra

Shakti Mudra

Benefits: Helps awaken creativity and passion, also helps heal trauma from abuse, including sexual abuse. Opens the connection with the cycles of nature. Helps to relieve insomnia, encourages feelings of safety and relaxation.

Shakti Mudra

Technique: Sit in a comfortable position, and with your palms in facing each other in front of your chest, press your pinky and ring fingertips together. Fold your thumbs into your palms and cover them with your index and middle fingers, pressing the knuckles of these fingers together. You can leave your hands here, or drop your hands in front of the navel area. Hold for 5 to 45 minutes, incorporating a mantra or an affirmation from this chapter if you like.

Guided Meditation

For a free recording of this meditation and other audios that you can listen to and follow along with, visit our special webpage for readers of this book: alyssamalehorn.com/ hoiys

Take a few deep breaths, and start to let the air flow all the way down into your belly. Relax your stomach and your hips, allowing yourself to fully breathe... slowly and gently. As you read this, say "Thank you" to all of your Divine helpers, guides, angels, and the Great Spirit.

Now you're going to invite in the energy that you need for your healing. Sense an orange light, coming from the heavens and filling your body. It's focusing and swirling around and in your belly area, just under your navel. This is an orange energy, but it's also the energy of flowing water. It's the energy of a stream or a creek. It can even feel or look in your mind like a soft waterfall. It's also the energy of the moonlight. What stage is your moon in? Is it a full moon, a crescent moon? What moon do you picture when you're pulling in that orange energy into that sacral area of your body? Just picture it. Just allow your senses to take it all in. Take a deep breath. You can let your mind relax.

Now you're going to address the things that you've stored in the sacral chakra—the things that you've stored through ancestral patterns, lineage issues, past lifetimes, and this lifetime. Up until this point, you've needed everything that you've stored in this chakra. Now you'll more consciously choose what you need and what you don't.

Everything you've stored in these chakras has also affected your cells, your organs, and your systems. It's affected you physically, mentally, emotionally, and spiritually. Now here you are, making conscious choices about what you want to include. So begin by giving thanks for all of the wisdom, love, and everything you've gotten either from this lifetime, other lifetimes, from your ancestors, or from your lineage.

Give thanks for everything you've learned from the challenging aspects, and from the obvious blessings; from some of the things that weren't so happy, and some of the things that were very happy. Give thanks for all of the wonderful things that have been brought to you, such as the energies of creativity and sensuality. As you give thanks, you're amplifying the positive energies, including the energies of nourishment, emotions, presence in the moment, and positive boundaries.

Give thanks to all of this, in all aspects of time and space, and in all aspects of you—physical, emotional, mental, ethereal, astral—in every possible way, including factors that are known to you, and factors that are unknown.

Now it's time to give thanks for and to release any and all of the following that are no longer serving you. You are now releasing those energies that you no longer need, either from this lifetime, past lifetimes, ancestral, and lineage issues. This includes any and all lack of acceptance of your physical body, self-judgment, self-criticism. You're neutralizing and releasing the energies of distraction, disconnection, fear of losing control, the energy of abuse and trauma, and the fear of being controlled. Breathe deeply and allow your fear of losing control to swirl and gently release from your belly area, down your legs, out through the bottoms of your feet and down deep into the Earth.

You're neutralizing and giving thanks for all of the lessons and everything that you've learned—all of the wisdom, and all of the love. And now, you will complete that releasing of any of these that you are no longer using, and any others that I did not mention that are not in your highest good, that you're no longer working with. As I count down from ten to one, you will release whatever you no longer need, whatever is no longer for your highest benefit, and is no longer helping you achieve your highest good and your own joy. As I count down from ten to one, you'll neutralize and release that. Ten, nine, eight, seven, six, five, four, three, two, one. Take a deep breath, and now release it. Perfect.

If you feel emotional, know that is okay; just let it keep flowing through. You're only releasing what your higher self has agreed to release, whatever you are done with.

Keep breathing. Imagine that you have deep roots coming from the base of your spine and the bottoms of your feet that go all the way down into the core of the Earth. These deep roots can be like tree roots; they can be like cables. Whatever they are, they're keeping you grounded, and centered, and reminding you of your sense of safety, your sense of security. That is real. You are safe. All is well.

Now you're going to create healing from all of your lifetimes as a second level child soul and as a child in this lifetime. Affirm: "I allow all appropriate, optimal, beneficial, and benevolent healing from all of my lifetimes as a second level child soul and in this lifetime, from the moment that I became eight years old until my final moment of age fourteen. I allow all of the appropriate, optimal, beneficial, and benevolent healing."

This is when you were learning energetically and spiritually all about control and influence. Your sacral chakra was waking up at this time. You were learning about control and influence over your environment, over your outcomes. Maybe you felt like you didn't have any control. Maybe you felt like you had no influence. You were learning all about that through contrast. You were learning about control of your own choices, your own rights, your own responsibilities, and your senses. This is when sensuality wakes up. You were learning about your influences and your communication—how what you say matters, and how what you don't say matters. It's all important. Take a deep breath.

All of the frequencies in your body right now are being harmonized. They're being optimized. Your glands, your organs, your systems, your blood, and all the water in your body—they're all being upgraded and optimized. As you close this healing meditation, you are giving thanks for the awareness of your own body, and we each embrace the optimal passion for life. Breath in that passion—the innate passion to live the life that you were meant to live, with joy, peace, creativity, and love, and more.

As you count down from ten to one, you'll allow this healing to take place. Ten, nine, eight, seven, six, five, four, three, two, one. Take a deep breath, and now exhale. Allow whatever comes to your mind, to come. All is well.

Just keep breathing. Be present in your body. There's no rush. You have plenty of time. When you're complete, stretch, take a deep breath, and write down some notes about what you've experienced.

Now you have a fully awakened, beautifully balanced, root and sacral chakra system. All of your other chakras are beginning their realignment and recalibration process in preparation for the next chapters. You may repeat this meditation as often as you like.

~ CHAPTER 5 ~

THE ADOLESCENT SOUL

"How wonderful it is that nobody need wait a single moment before starting to improve the world." ~ Anne Frank

THERE ARE MORE LEVEL THREE, ADOLESCENT SOULS on the planet now than any other soul age. They've been in the majority since the mid-1990s, and now about fifty percent of the population on Earth are adolescent or teenage souls. As you can imagine, when we have a majority of a specific soul age, the influence that they have on society and our culture is enormous.

Much like we do when we're teens in physical form, most teenage souls are drawn to chaos and activity. This is one of the reasons that teenage souls are attracted to city life. Visit any big busy city, and you'll find a majority of teenage souls. Throughout the course of this book, you'll notice that people in some of the other soul ages (infant, child, and old souls) don't typically gravitate toward big cities. They could love the energy of the city for a visit, but it would be difficult, tiring, and draining for these types of souls to live full-time in a fast-moving, noisy, chaotic city for too long. Many do, and don't realize it's the city energy that's weighing them down.

Creativity

Adolescent/young adult souls are usually very creative, and they express themselves well. You'll see lots of folks in this third phase of soul development if you just turn on the television on any given day. A lot of the people you see on movies and TV (especially reality shows) and many of the people who are behind the scenes, creating that media, are in this level.

These are the people who not only have an idea of how to get money, attention and fame, but they actually put action behind it and get it done. It's only in the early stages of the adolescent soul phase that they tend to feel entitled to fame or money. When they've progressed beyond that early stage, they are usually very hardworking. That's one of the gifts of this soul age, they can set goals and reach them, and if they're in the harmonious part of this stage, they won't let anything stop them.

> *"The question isn't who is going to let me; it's who is going to stop me."* ~ Ayn Rand

Yes, we have creatives in every soul phase, but the talent that comes from the level three souls can be super impressive. So many of them are willing to do the work and really learn their craft to become the best because of the energy from the development of the solar plexus chakra, where the strength of the will develops. It's the adolescent soul's true nature to express themselves in a big way.

Look at Me!

This soul wants to be seen and heard, all of the time. When this is out of balance, narcissism can take over, and this is common in this soul growth stage. It's the "look at me" stage, where there's more effort and concern put into how things *look*, as opposed to how they actually *are*. The 24-hour social-media-involvement pattern plays into the heart of these souls. Most adolescent souls need to be connected and have some admiration almost constantly. Their self-worth relies on the opinions of other people. We wouldn't have Photoshop or selfies if it weren't for teenage souls.

Compare the ability of the adolescent soul to craft their image, to a child soul who hasn't had even one thought about how they appear, except they assume it's positive because they are "right" or righteous. An older soul many times won't have any idea of how they appear, simply because it's less important to them. The young adolescent soul will commonly craft an image of material success and happiness, even if they haven't achieved either of those things.

Some of the narcissism in teenage or adolescent souls can be used to their advantage, to be able to move into the more positive aspects of the "I." "How can I fix this? How can I improve myself? How can I help?" Engaging in charitable work is one of the best things that level three souls can do to help them along their spiritual journey. The key is to find something they love, that they feel is important, and then use that wonderful energy and action that is so common in this group to help. We require the passion of teenage souls to move causes forward, and they can bring a wonderful momentum with their natural energy.

If a level three teenage soul can find and access that charitable aspect within themselves and put their passion into it, they are developing their soul in leaps and bounds. As they're moving forward, they won't fail to remind you of the good work they've done, and they might even bring it up again and again. However, they can be naturally generous, and when they've grown a little spiritually, they don't require as much attention for their giving.

Even if they feel they must get credit or be honored for the good deeds they pursue, even if they're doing the charitable work to get attention and approval, that energy will still help them move into the next phase, where there is less inner and outer chaos, less drama in relationships, and generally more peace and emotional freedom. The charitable aspect within these souls is wonderful, and these souls can really help people and the environment.

Looking Within

Introspection isn't the level three soul's forte. They are more concerned with the way they are seen than who they really are. The narcissistic aspect of this soul age can easily get out of control and can become quite manipulative, typically without even realizing it. In this case, it's not a conscious decision to manipulate a person or situation; they just want to make sure that no one's forgetting about them, and they are trying to manage their fear of abandonment and deeper feelings of unworthiness. Of course, humans in every soul level can have these same issues, and if you feel like an older soul and you experience some of these "symptoms," it's a sure sign that you have some unresolved issues from when you were a level three adolescent soul.

If you identify with that, recall the previous section about charitable giving and find something you can put your heart into. As you focus on giving time, talents or energy, you'll notice that the rest of your life starts to calm down a little bit. Your soul is responding to the heart connection of your giving, which is helping you find balance in every possible way.

Depression and anxiety are prevalent in this soul level, especially when they feel like they're not getting enough appropriate attention from others. The way to resolve this, whether you are a teenage soul or not, is to give yourself the amount of attention and self-love that you need, rather than look externally for approval. Part of the learning experience for all souls is to understand when to focus on self-care, especially when you feel like you're not getting what you need from other people, if you're feeling victimized or let down. The deeper lesson within that scenario is the self-questioning, "Did my actions worsen the situation?" or "How could I have improved this for everyone involved?"

Like younger souls, adolescent souls can also tend to blame other people or external circumstances for their problems. If you're an adolescent soul, if all of this is really making sense to you, one of your biggest soul lessons is to be able to look inward and be able to ask yourself, "What is it that I can do to help my situation?" The habit of looking outside of yourself for someone to help you or to rescue you or to take care of you will be outgrown in time. Your job is to begin to look inward, to begin to acknowledge your spirit, and find the quiet inside.

Passion and Fear

What I love most about these souls is their passion. When they believe in something, they are going to shout it from the rooftops or, for the modern day equivalent, they'll post it online. If you need a marketer, grab an adolescent soul and turn them on to your business! They're natural marketers and networkers.

Adolescent souls bring a sense of passion and excitement to the planet. On their best days, they can be dynamic and very committed to what they're doing. They are typically motivated, enthusiastic, and go-getters. The movers and shakers of the world are usually in this soul group. However, their energy is often focused on external gratification, such as money, power, attention, and material things. They can be collectors, where they'll tend to accumulate lots of stuff and friends, whether they truly like them or not. If they're honest with themselves, they'll see that they collect because they're concerned about how they believe they'll be perceived, above anything else.

Adolescent souls commonly fear being judged, based on their appearance. You know you're in this soul level if you are consistently pre-occupied with how you look, how you dress, or have fear that you're always being sized-up by other people. It's normal to want to look attractive and appealing, but with these souls, the fear of judgment can be overwhelming, much like how an adolescent can become consumed by how other people view them. Toward the end of this soul level, these feelings will evolve into discovering how you can feel good and get admiration from within. At that point, they can reach a temporarily satisfying level of accomplishment, wealth or attractiveness.

The inner conflict that level three souls are trying to resolve involves a triad of deep beliefs that are all fighting for dominance. The first belief is a remnant from their lifetimes as a level two child soul. It's a belief that being different is bad and dangerous. The second is a fear that they aren't good enough to stand alone, a holdover from their lifetimes as a level one infant soul. The third player in this inner conflict is the deep feeling of longing to be different and stand out, with a desire to prove that they are indeed good enough (rich enough, pretty enough, smart enough, successful enough). This is the new, level three idea. These three aspects push against each other until the phase is complete and the soul has matured into a new state of awareness.

If you feel that you're resonating with this struggle, you'll find tools at the end of this chapter to help you move through this phase, whether you're an adolescent soul or an older soul with unresolved level three issues.

Fear of boredom is pervasive in this soul age. Their minds are always seeking stimulation and distraction. It's a very different type of stimulus-seeking than any other group's, because they are looking for something to react to or respond to, not just looking to be entertained (although that's certainly part of it). There's a desire for involvement that comes in at this level. Social media was created *by* people in this soul phase, *for* people in this soul phase, providing unlimited opportunities to be involved with anyone and everything through posting online comments, pictures, and votes.

There are lots of sports fans in this level. They like to be united in a cause or a sport, and they can be very loyal fans, even when their team isn't performing well. They may be disappointed, but they typically aren't going to give up on their team. The glue that holds them together is something tangible; usually its geography, with them all living in the same area or originally being from the same hometown. The energy of competition makes sense to them and cooperation within a team is something they love to be part of, even if it's from the sidelines.

Spotlight and Power

As you might imagine, there are many celebrities, politicians and CEOs in this group. You can identify the adolescent souls from older souls by the way they seek and use the spotlight. The adolescent soul will seek the spotlight first, and then decide how to use the power/fame/money/status that comes to them through having attained it. Sometimes there's no other goal, other than admiration or perceived power. The older soul will have a plan to help others, once success is evident. With the older souls, there's a higher purpose intended for the money or fame that they seek. Certainly every wealthy, driven, or famous person isn't an adolescent soul. They're just in the majority in those environments. The older souls in those arenas are helping to balance the energy, whether they're consciously aware of it or not.

Adolescent souls have an innate desire for power and success, because they are seeing the world through the lens of the solar plexus chakra. This means that they are mastering the art of getting things done, and at the same time, they are learning how to connect their hearts to their work. The solar plexus chakra (just above the navel of the body) is the seat of your will forces. It's about being proactive, and noticing if your proactivity is motivated by fear, or motivated by love. The ideal would be to link proactivity to love, and when you've done so, your heart chakra is connected to your efforts. This helps your soul to move forward and continue to develop into the next levels.

The solar plexus chakra is the seat of our willpower and ability to allow ourselves to be seen. We develop this chakra during our adolescent soul lifetimes, and in this current lifetime, between the ages of 15 and 21 and again between the ages of 64 and 70. Through this energy center, we learn how to use the strength of our will to take action, how to be reliable and responsible, and how to use our personal power. The personality and the ego are formed in this chakra, and we must fully understand those aspects to have a healthy solar plexus. When this chakra is in need of repair, the issues of the adolescent level soul present themselves, regardless of our soul's age. These issues can manifest as an inability to relax into life, perpetually feeling stressed out, over- or under-emphasizing personal power, over- or under-reacting to life's circumstances, and a general inability to find balance. Use the tools at the end of this chapter to begin healing those wounds.

The solar plexus is the follow-through chakra. If you have trouble finishing what you've started, or don't seem to have any willpower, you're working with solar plexus energy. You might be an adolescent soul, or you might be an older soul healing from when you were an adolescent soul. You can remember that the solar plexus is the chakra that these younger souls are working with so diligently, because of the "solar" part of the name: it refers to the sun that shines forth from within, and we see that positive characteristic in most teen souls.

True, there can be laziness in any of the soul ages, but it's rare in the later stages of the adolescent/young adult age. Laziness and entitlement are more pervasive in the early part of this phase. With the frequency on the planet right now changing and improving so much, we are going to be seeing less and less of that entitlement energy and personality focus, and more of the positive aspects of this soul age.

Teen souls also tend to struggle with a double standard regarding habits and willpower. If a level three soul smokes cigarettes, they'll tend to overlook the health concerns in favor of their belief, "It's a bad habit, but I could be doing worse things." But if a level three soul is allergic to smoke, they will tend to see smokers as being weak-willed for having a habit that they perceive as negative.

Relationships

> *"I'm selfish, impatient and a little insecure. I make mistakes, I am out of control and at times hard to handle. But if you can't handle me at my worst, then you sure as hell don't deserve me at my best."* ~ Marilyn Monroe

These souls can also be much more fickle than younger or older souls. They can easily move from one passion to the next, and the same goes for their relationships. There isn't a lot of healing time between relationships or marriages, and they can have several significant relationships in a single lifetime.

Infidelity most often occurs in this level and the child soul phase (and if an older soul is healing wounds from these phases). It's not that they have no conscience; it's that other things (such as getting attention and feeling admired) can be more important than their loved ones' feelings or expectations. What feels good now takes precedence over what would feel good for the long term. In love relationships and in other areas of their life, this soul can have challenges with maintaining a long-term vision with regard to possible consequences.

When adolescent souls marry outside of their soul age group, it can eventually become problematic. It's difficult for an adolescent/young adult soul to put someone else on the same level as themselves. They tend to either want to be superior or want others to support them—emotionally, physically, and even spiritually. How do they move through that energy and have a happy marriage or partnership, where both people feel and are equally important? It requires development of the heart chakra while balancing the other chakras, which comes more easily in the older soul phases. In this situation, allowing more light into the spiritual and physical bodies is the key. If you're an older soul married to a younger soul, the following chapters will give you the information you need to better understand the dynamics.

In earlier chapters, I mentioned that the infant-level souls typically haven't developed empathy and child souls are just beginning to learn it throughout that level. Empathy is just starting to really take root in the adolescent/young adult level. They're able to access deep levels of empathy and love as they near the later phases of this level, as they move closer to the heart chakra. This is one of the reasons that some of our most prolific actors can "become" the character they're playing. If they've connected with that heart energy and created harmony with the solar plexus, they can be transformative creatives.

They can be much more open minded than younger souls, and tend to develop a live-and-let-live attitude when it comes to sexual orientation, politics, etc. Part of this trait is because of their newly acquired connection with their heart chakra and some of it can be because of their self-absorption: "I don't care what you do as long as it doesn't negatively impact me."

I love the openness that wakes up in adolescent souls. They are open to experiment with new ideas, music styles, and they are frequently willing to make mistakes and see the mistake as part of their process. Fear of failure doesn't typically stop folks in this realm, and neither does fear of success. If they're in the later stages of level three, they are usually willing to risk it; they'll keep on plugging away until they reach their goals or until they graduate to the next soul level, where they won't feel the same drive for acceptance based on achievement.

Extremes

There can be a penchant for extremes, like workaholism, alcohol, sex, and drug addictions, mainly because the solar plexus is activated but isn't yet balanced, and the new, deeply felt heart dynamics can be hard to deal with. Experiencing empathy can be painful and too much to bear for many in this soul group, so there's a tendency to want to numb out. Other reasons for excesses and addiction in this group include the habits of self-judgment and being on an emotional roller coaster. They are a lot like physical adolescents and young adults in that way.

Charisma, idealism, youthful vitality and energy are common in this group. They tend to claw their way to the top, acquiring either accolades or a trail of broken hearts behind them. These souls haven't yet developed their gentleness of heart, and their egos are mostly in control. Remember that the ego is the mind's identity, which regularly compares ourselves to others and decides who's better or worse, who's worthy and who's not. As we become more mature soul-wise, we can see the ego for what it is and just observe its ramblings, instead of buying into what it's telling us. An older soul can tell the difference between the ego and the truth, whereas a level three soul tends to believe what the ego is saying, and they also believe that what they think is who they are.

These souls aren't too spiritually introspective, although there is a curiosity there. They aren't usually devoutly religious, but they can be spiritual. If they're religious, it's because it feels good to belong, not necessarily because it feels right. The main reason an adolescent soul would be introspective is if they were rejected or abandoned and they would only look inward after exhausting all of the other reasons that the other person was wrong. An older soul would look inward first and blame themselves; a younger soul wouldn't look inward at all, and the adolescent soul has the maturity to eventually get there, but not without first engaging in an internal struggle.

Remember, it's normal for an actual teenager to have some or most of these qualities. The age of the *soul* becomes more apparent when we are around the physical ages of 35–40. If these traits are still the norm at those ages, it's more indicative of an adolescent soul.

What Can't They Do?

One of the questions that comes to mind about those souls is, "What *can't* they do?" That's the overall, no-limits feeling. With the energy of the Earth supporting them as they naturally mature, I predict that the adolescent/young adult souls will be solving our environmental issues. I imagine they'll be re-inventing our transportation system and, when they're almost to the next soul level, they'll be solving the problems of hunger and disease. I love the positive energy that they can bring, even if chaos sometimes follows them because of the unrest in their inner world.

They embody the "I can do it" attitude and also the "just do it" way of life. They are the do-ers right now, more than any other soul group. As long as they're working on their own soul development, they'll get to a calmer place as time goes on. It'll still be full of action, but with some peace of mind thrown in—more cooperation and less of that individual "look at me" energy.

Adolescent souls who are attracted to sports (and there are many) can shine brightly and make a name for themselves. Think of someone—an athlete who trains, excels, and dedicates his life to his sport, but who also compromises himself by wanting to win at any cost, even if it means using performance-enhancing drugs. That's a good example of a level three soul that can easily slip out of balance into extremes, and eventually into chaos. You can see how the extremes can appear to be a huge benefit, because they support great success and accomplishment. The chaos that follows is typical, whether on a small, private scale or a large, public scale.

The energy and drive starts out very pure. Then (because the solar plexus and the heart chakra aren't yet in harmony) the intense drive—to win, be admired or be the best—overtakes the person's better judgment and character. The heart chakra is the bridge between the lower, more survival-based energy centers and the upper, more spiritual centers. The heart feeds both and provides a connection between our spiritual selves and our human selves. When the solar plexus is still in development, the influence of the heart chakra is minimal, and that's when you see these types of issues.

What an incredible journey these level three souls are on! They are opening and intensifying the solar plexus chakra like they never have before, in any other lifetime, and they're starting to touch the heart in brand new ways, as well. The heart energy is still more connected to the lower chakras than the upper ones, which can mean that generosity, love and compassion can tend to be conditional at this soul age: "I love you, as long as you love me," and "I'll give charitably, as long as you're doing it my way and I get credit."

I've mentioned before that there are spiritual teachers at every soul level. The adolescent soul age teachers are charismatic, like the child soul teachers, but far less condemning. They are more focused on open-mindedness, positive reinforcement, reminding you of your worth, and helping to awaken your ability to receive love. They can push the prosperity teachings, such as "the law of attraction." They want everyone to be successful, but only if they don't get outshone! "Will it minimize me if you're successful?" It's a real concern for these souls.

These souls don't tend to take long breaks between lifetimes. The life-between-lives recuperation is pretty quick for adolescent souls. They're ambitious and ready for the next challenge.

The overall growth during adolescent soul lifetimes will be focused on the issues that originate in the solar plexus chakra, including:

- Lack of consistent empathy
- Narcissism
- Feeling superior or greatly inferior, difficult to find balance
- More motivated by money, power, admiration, or sexual pleasure than by harmony
- Create challenging, dramatic situations, especially in relationships
- Limit themselves spiritually, by only having interest in the spiritual or psychological trend of the moment, rather than by noticing what's really working for them
- Not having peace of mind as a goal: material things, pleasure or reputation are often more important
- Strings are often attached to their giving
- "Retaliation is more honorable than forgiveness."
- Make decisions based on unresolved fear or feeling victimized
- Lots of fear of being seen as wrong
- Struggles with will power

The most positive, wonderful aspects of this soul age include:

- Enthusiasm and passion
- Ability to learn quickly
- Motivated to make an impact
- Not afraid of attention or the limelight
- New innovations and ideas commonly arise from this group

- Tech and other lifestyle improvements
- Fashion, style, music, trends, and social networking are all important to them; they influence society through these means
- Can become very empathetic and caring in the later stages
- Strengthening of the will forces, the ability to "power-through"
- Can be very charitable and generous, even when doing it for attention, respect or appreciation
- "Fire in the belly" type of passion for whatever is believed in

If you feel like you're an older soul, and yet you see yourself in some of these teenage soul traits, you can know that you're working on healing your solar plexus chakra from the wounds that are still unhealed from when you were an adolescent soul. In this lifetime, these issues will have originally manifested most obviously during the ages of 15 to 21. They can continue to plague you as time goes on, if they remain unhealed.

How do you know if you have unhealed issues from when you were a level three soul that resulted in issues in this lifetime that arose during the ages of 15 to 21, or 64 to 70?

- If you have trouble releasing judgment of self and others
- If you crave the spotlight and it feels like an unhealthy obsession
- If you're overly concerned with how you look and how you'll be judged by others

- If you have charitable, generous feelings but getting credit is as important than the cause
- If you find yourself looking for ways to get attention, regardless of what you have to do
- If you are addicted to social media
- If you have a hard time finishing projects that you start
- If you regularly find yourself on an emotional roller coaster
- If you fantasize about or seek revenge when you feel wronged
- If you feel superior one minute and inferior the next
- If you put yourself in stressful situations in an attempt to keep up with the perceived material success of others
- If receiving admiration is a concern for you

Here are your tools to help you heal and move forward!

Affirmations

I love and accept myself fully.

I express myself clearly and easily.

I am in my personal power.

I choose what's best for me and I direct my own life.

I am worthy of love and acceptance.

Centering

Close your eyes and put your hands on your belly area, just above your navel. Imagine there's a small, golden pinpoint of light in your belly. As you breathe naturally, allow that golden pinpoint of light to grow bigger and brighter with every breath. It becomes as bright as the sunshine on a perfect summer afternoon. Allow the glowing sunshine to shine brightly within you and all around you. Stay in this energy as long as you like. Anytime you feel unbalanced or in need of willpower or self-control, return to this centering vision.

Mantra

Ram (sounds like Rahm, elongating the RAAH sound gently into the AHMM)

or

any of the affirmations above

For a free recording of these mantras and other audios that you can listen to and gain the benefits from, even while you sleep, visit our special webpage for readers of this book: alyssamalehorn.com/hoiys

~ ~ ~

Mudra

Prana Mudra

Prana Mudra

Benefits: strengthens energy field. It increases overall strength and feelings of wellbeing, helps to create a seal around the energy field. Strengthens willpower, vitality, immunity. Great to use when you're exhausted or feel energetically vulnerable. On each hand, cover the tips of the ring and little fingers with the thumb, extend the middle and index fingers. Rest your hands in your lap or fingers pointing upward, hands resting against the sides of the abdomen. Hold for 5 to 45 minutes, incorporating a mantra or an affirmation from this chapter if you like, or visualizing the golden, sunny light from the belly area, as in the preceding centering exercise.

Guided Meditation

Take a few deep breaths, and start to let the air flow all the way down into your belly. Relax your stomach and your hips, allowing yourself to breathe fully ... slowly and gently. As you read this, say "Thank you" to all of your Divine helpers, guides, angels, and the Great Spirit.

Now you're going to invite in the energy that you need for your healing. Just take some deep breaths. This is your time now. You can leave all of your worries behind. Nobody needs anything from you right now. You can just allow yourself to relax into the flow of this moment and just keep breathing. Whatever comes into your mind is just right for you. Any intrusive thoughts that come in while you're doing this...they're supposed to be there. Don't judge them; just let them move through. If you notice any sounds, just acknowledge them and let them go. This is your time.

Now let your breathing go into a normal, relaxed, rhythmic breath. Now you're going to tell your body to relax. Let your feet and legs soften into the position they're in, relax your hands, allow your shoulders to drop, and allow your full body to soften down and relax into a natural, comfortable position. Take another deep breath. Now you're going to allow your head and face to relax, your scalp, your forehead, all the tiny muscles around your eyes, your jaw, your muscles around your mouth—just let them all soften and relax. Take a cleansing breath in and, on your exhale breathe out all of the tension in your body. Now you can allow your breathing to fall into its own natural rhythm again. Don't try to control it in any way; just observe it. You're breathing relaxation in, and you're breathing tension out. If any thoughts flow into your mind, just allow them to flow on past.

I want you to bring your attention to your belly area. Imagine that you have a beautiful sunny yellow light there in your belly, just above your navel, and it's glowing like a fiery sun. Just notice how that feels, how it looks in your mind's eye, and feel the warmth growing in your midsection.

Focus back onto the sunshine in your belly. As this sunny glow expands in your abdomen, notice that it starts to gently spread out and get bigger as you breathe. It's a beautiful yellow color. Whatever yellow color comes to your mind is just the right color. Now draw your attention back to your breath, and as you breathe in, just imagine that you're breathing in more of that golden light. With every in-breath, you're pulling in more of that sunny light.

In these next few breaths, you're going to let that golden glow spread out into your whole body. It's going to go down into your arms and hands, down into your torso, into your legs, all the way down into your toes. Every breath you take in, you're breathing in more light... it's coming up into your chest, up into your head, it's connecting with all of your other chakras, and you're just filled with it.

Draw your attention back to your abdomen area, into the center of that golden light. As you breathe in this light, it's bringing you insight, self-love, and strength of will. While you're working in that space, you're going to neutralize some of the non-beneficial energies that may be residing there, in your solar plexus energy center. These may be thoughtforms, they may be residue, they may be patterns—anything that you're no longer learning from, that you no longer need, that's no longer beneficial—you're going to neutralize those energies now and release them, and then you will replace them consciously with some energies that you choose.

Right now, as you continue to breathe gently into your belly, you're going to go ahead and give thanks for all of the energies that are no longer serving you. You're giving thanks and recognizing that they're no longer needed. You're now neutralizing the energies of narcissism, abandonment, lack of compassion, lack of vitality, and fear. Take a deep breath, and you'll also neutralize the energy of old injuries or illness, any issues with the stomach, digestion issues, food allergies, sensitivities—you'll neutralize all of the non-beneficial energies that are there. Any residue from surgeries, injuries, any residue of feeling unimportant or unaccepted, you neutralize those as well. You neutralize the energies of lack of confidence and willpower. You'll neutralize all of those energies. Any other thoughts of non-beneficial issues that come to your mind, you're neutralizing them as well. Whether it's a lack of love, the energy of unwillingness or resistance, fear... you neutralize all of that now. You're deleting and un-creating those energies within you, from this lifetime, from any other lifetime, from all time, space, dimensions and realities.

Now say silently, in your mind, "I allow this healing." With a deep breath, now you invite in and give thanks for a new upgraded, fresh set of energies to fill your solar plexus center. You will invite in and give thanks for the energies of intelligence, confidence, willpower, compassion, focus, personality, and vitality. You invite in and give thanks for the energy of freedom, as your soul remembers that as its natural state.

So now you're going to create healing from all of your lifetimes as a third level child adolescent soul and as a teen in this lifetime. Affirm: "I allow all appropriate, optimal, beneficial, and benevolent healing from all of my lifetimes as a third level adolescent soul and from this lifetime, from the moment that I became 15 years old until my final moment of age 21. I allow all of the appropriate, optimal, beneficial, and benevolent healing."

Just focus on your breath. In your mind, say silently, "I allow this healing. I allow vitality and confidence. I allow all self-loathing to be completely dissolved." Now focus your attention on your belly again and feel that wonderful sunny glow; it's still gently radiating. With your next breath, you're breathing in that golden light, and you're breathing out tension.

Whenever you're ready, you can gently move your shoulders a little bit, start to be more aware of the room around you, and open your eyes. You now have a fully awakened, beautifully balanced, root, sacral, and solar plexus chakra system. All of your other chakras are beginning their realignment and recalibration process, in preparation for the next chapters. You may repeat this meditation as often as you like.

"Your role is to hold the energy of unconditional love, fully understanding that you have no idea what experiences other people have agreed to and attracted to themselves in an effort to complete their own soul's development."

~ CHAPTER 6 ~

MATURE SOULS

"Darkness cannot drive out darkness: only light can do that. Hate cannot drive out hate: only love can do that." ~ Martin Luther King Jr., *A Testament of Hope: The Essential Writings and Speeches*

LET'S MOVE INTO MATURE SOULS. This is the fourth out of the five main soul development stages. The focus is overwhelmingly on the heart. The mature soul is discovering that the heart is the center of our inner human universe. The importance of one's emotional life is starting to become apparent, little by little. This shows up in the mature soul's life in interesting ways. Sometimes it looks like a desire to create a life experience that's wonderfully heart-centered, and sometimes it looks like a perpetual running away from any depth of feeling at all.

At this level, there's an intense responsibility: to understand the heart's role more deeply. Most people won't fully complete this education during their lifetimes as a mature soul, but they'll start the process. Everything will gel in their older soul lifetimes, if they haven't completely mastered the heart connection. We're not just talking about the emotional heart (the feelings and emotions). The physical heart is a huge part of this developing picture. The human heart has a magnetic field that can be measured several feet away from the body. Those magnetic fields change, depending on how you feel emotionally, as do your immune system and nervous system.

The next step is realizing how that magnetic field affects you and the living things around you. You're radiating a crystal clear message directly from your heart to every person around you, with a ripple effect throughout the collective consciousness in the world. Understanding and taking responsibility for that message is a huge aspect of the mature soul's journey. If the facts aren't understood about each human's ability to choose positive emotions over painful or negative emotions, then mature souls can live in a state of either emotional overwhelm or shutdown. When you feel as though you have no control over your feelings, and you then allow them to run rampant in response to life's events, it makes sense that that the out-of-control energy would cause some pretty desperate reactions. It's interesting to note that mature souls are far more sensitive to other people's emotions than those in the previous soul levels. Those magnetic waves of energy (that are coded with emotions) that we all broadcast, are also received, loud and clear.

> *Emotional information is actually coded and modulated into these fields. By learning to shift our emotions, we are changing the information coded into the magnetic fields that are radiated by the heart, and that can impact those around us. We are fundamentally and deeply connected with each other and the planet itself.* ~ Rolin McCratey PhD, director of research at the Heart Math Institute

Most of us believe that when the brain experiences something, it then sends a signal to the heart, and then we experience the emotion, but scientific studies tell us otherwise. The heart is receiving impulses and information, and then sending the signal to the brain, far more often than the other way around. The heart knows many things before the brain has any idea of them. (You can find the research at https://www.heartmath.org/)

Negative emotions, such as jealousy and worry, depress the immune system and cause chaos in the nervous system; positive emotions boost the immune system and balance the nervous system. It's as simple as that. When you truly believe that you have a choice when it comes to how you feel, and that positive emotions can be generated through practices like meditation, singing, dancing, being in nature or with animals, you're working with the flow of your curriculum as an evolving soul, instead of against it.

Mature or adult souls tend to have a good understanding of other people's perspectives. Early in this level, their "live and let live" philosophy usually extends only to people that they know, not so much to people that they aren't closely involved with. They're learning how to extend that attitude to all of life. As they move through the sub-levels within the mature soul level, they'll begin to project the energy of all-inclusive acceptance.

They can be more open-minded than adolescent souls; there is a lot of caring in this level, and a more liberal view of life than in any of the earlier levels. There is a strong desire to connect emotionally and socially, because mature souls are intensely developing the heart chakra. In this level, the development and refining of the heart chakra is like the blossoming of a beautiful flower. It's fragile and unique, all the while providing beauty and gentleness to all who connect there.

When we're newly experiencing life through the lens of the heart, the risk of heartbreak and holding onto resentment can be huge. The ability to become vulnerable starts to awaken, and there's a deeper access to the heart in general. While it can feel scary and overwhelming at times, this vulnerability is a marker of the newfound strength of the heart. As a bonus for all of this heart work, we get to experience a deeper level of compassion and generosity at the same time.

It goes without saying that souls in all stages of development feel love, generosity and compassion, but for the level four, adult/mature soul, it's the new-found depth that's captivating. They show compassion one minute, and then analyze why they felt that way in the next. The origin of their beliefs and feelings have been hidden and somewhat of a mystery in the previous soul levels, so there is a curiosity about what would make them feel one way or the other. The vast exploration of the heart has officially begun.

Feeling So Much, So Deeply

Unresolved issues in the lower energy centers typically begin to arise at this level in soul development. Many times, these unhealed wounds from past incarnations will start to surface in the form of chronic illness or discomfort. Weight issues and addictions are common in this level because, for the first time, the mature soul is feeling everything on such a deep level and it can be overwhelming. When you first begin to feel deeply into the heart, the internalizing mechanism kicks in, and you bury your feelings into the psyche and deeply into the cells and systems of the body. This, of course, isn't a sustainable long-term plan and it causes problems down the road if those feelings aren't addressed, like the saying goes: "Feelings buried alive never die." Part of the path of the mature soul is to dig up the old feelings, allow them to flow through and be acknowledged, and then release them to make room for a better way of being.

Even good feelings can be too much to handle. Too much love, acceptance, happiness or success can throw the level four soul off balance to the point where they want to numb out. It's true that even if it's not necessarily a painful feeling, it can be overwhelming just by its depth or magnitude. We see this many times in people who have a quick rise to the top, whether it's in business or performance or another field. The adjustment from feeling the energy of struggle on a regular basis to feeling exalted or successful can be just too much. Addiction, health issues, and emotional imbalances are good examples of the repercussions of this dynamic. The tools at the end of this chapter can help you create a bridge from struggle to success, without invoking the intense challenges.

Many of my clients are in the mature and old soul phases, and they usually seek help and find me when they feel like they've suffered long enough. They'll say, "I am just so tired of feeling overwhelmed (or guilty, or sad, or tired)" This brings up the issue of the suffering of the mature soul. Along with the energies of love and generosity, the heart chakra holds the energy of suffering when it's not harmonized well with the other chakras. Level fours can tend to suffer in silence for a long time before they finally start to engage the energy of the throat chakra to speak up. And when they open that door, look out! They've been silent for too long and they're not holding back. Tact isn't a strong suit at this level. Mature souls won't fully hone that throat chakra expression energy until they move into the older soul realm, but it's important to start the process when it feels right to do so.

Emotional withdrawal isn't a long-term solution to deal with the overwhelming heart energy that's starting to emerge in this phase. It does seem to be one of the more common techniques, but it wears out its welcome over time, as soul growth continues. Many of you reading this book identify with this, as the majority of those attracted to these teachings will be levels four and five, mature and old souls. The energy transmissions and the understanding you'll receive from this book will help you understand how you feel, why you feel that way, and how to feel better.

The heart chakra is the center of love and compassion. We develop this chakra during our mature soul lifetimes and, in this current lifetime, between the ages of 22 and 28, and again between the ages of 71 and 77. When this energy center is developing, we start to sense a deeper connection between ourselves and every other living thing. We feel things more deeply and are looking for ways to communicate our love, generosity and acceptance—

not just of others, but ourselves as well. When this chakra is out of balance, the most obvious sign is emotional withdrawal or closed-off energy. The less obvious (but just as important) symptoms include a lack of self-love and self-acceptance. The tools at the end of this chapter can help you open your heart to others and to yourself, in a clearer, more accepting way.

"I just feel everything so deeply," the mature soul says, and it's true. Feel, feel, feel! That's the word of this stage, until harmony becomes equally important. In the earlier stage of level four they feel deeply, quietly, withdrawn. While still feeling deeply, mature souls gradually start to express their distrust of government, corporations, their ex, their mom, themselves or whomever. When you reach the point where you're willing to discuss how you feel and share your heart in that way, without resisting your own peace, you're then inviting the energy of harmony and moving forward on your way through this stage, preparing for your entrance into the older soul stage.

The creativity and expression that's awakening within the throat chakra can inspire the late-stage mature soul to begin to communicate how they feel. Balance in that throat chakra doesn't come with the territory yet, but intensity surely does. The mature soul isn't feeling things a little; it's a lot and it's most all of the time, unless they're numbing out with substances, exercise or some other attempt to control the (perceived) out-of-control development that's going on. There can be a duality between emotional rigidity and hyperflexibility in this stage. One minute, they desperately want everything and everyone to be okay, and will try to control everything in an effort to make that happen. The next minute, they're so flexible with their boundaries that they're unsure of what they even care about. We could call it the "If I can't control it, then forget it" syndrome.

The new, deep feelings of empathy and heart connection can be so intertwined with the throat chakra that the polarity of control/rigidity (not wanting to compromise at all, in an effort to feel safe) and withdrawal/hyperflexibility (never speaking up on their own behalf, in an effort to maintain harmony) is enormous.

You know you're an evolving level four soul when you are willing to look at and uncover your deepest feelings, work on resolving them, and are eventually willing to forgive. Here's the disclaimer about forgiveness, though: the mature soul tends to hold on to some resentment for a while because that anger helps them feel less like a victim. It's not a bad thing to allow yourself to feel anger. The feeling of anger only becomes toxic when you're holding on to it beyond the length of time that it's helping you feel stronger. Souls in the next phase (old souls) typically go through that pattern too, but they tend to release it after the ages 40 to 45, whereas mature souls can hold a grudge their entire lives.

Mature souls really want to get to the bottom of how they feel and why they feel that way. Then, they'll want to help you figure out how you feel and why. Getting to the root of these issues for themselves and others is a goal in this level, with the ultimate goal being the alleviation of suffering. As you might imagine, many psychologists and other mental health professionals are in this stage, wanting to help their clients analyze their feelings, as they vicariously participate in their process.

This can be a difficult stage, as I suppose they all can be at different times. The challenge here lies more in the blessing or curse (depending on how you look at it) of being able to feel so deeply. Having this type of access to the heart can feel like a curse until the constant inflow and outflow of feelings are transformed from suffering to love.

Fitting In

One of the challenges that mature souls (and the next level, older souls) face is feeling like they don't fit in, don't know where they belong, and feeling like they're just not really sure how to express themselves. It's interesting to note that they are becoming routinely accepting of other people's differences, and yet they can have such a hard time with their own. They can sometimes feel as though they don't fit in, can feel like they were born in the wrong time or era, or they can feel fed up with the way the planet is right now. For mature souls, part of the exploration is finding where they fit, how they can serve, and what a wonderful role they play.

You'll see in the next chapter that older souls can also feel like they don't know where they belong, but there's a big difference between the way the level four and the level five souls experience this. The level four mature soul will make changes to themselves so they can fit in. They'll sacrifice something they believe in to make sure they have a group. Level five old souls are unable to make that sacrifice, and they don't attach the same level of importance to fitting in or belonging. You'll find more about that in the next chapter.

Mature souls typically have some trouble deciding on a career and finding out what they want to contribute to the planet. They can also feel like they have a whole bunch of different interests, as can adolescent souls, but with mature souls the primary approach is, "I have all of these great interests, but I'm just not sure exactly which one is going to help people more." with the secondary thought, "Which one is going to make me happier?" Mature souls are learning how to take care of their own needs. They can tend to give too much and can have huge amounts of empathy, because they're outgrowing the "us and them" mentality. They are moving into the belief that we are all in this together.

Just as these souls can indefinitely hold onto anger toward someone who's wronged them, they can also blame themselves in the same way. The tendency is toward self-blame for every little thing, and then turning that blame into an assault on their own character. They're learning how to accurately perceive what is truly their responsibility, and what they're unnecessarily taking on from others.

To move forward spiritually, mature souls need to become aware of that tendency. They tend to be the worst critics of themselves, and can turn that into intense perfectionism. While someone in any soul development phase can be a perfectionist, a mature soul can stop themselves from doing new things or expressing creativity, for fear of not being perfect. It can put the brakes on their expression and slow their creative development, as well as their soul evolution.

Perfectionism is also the culprit in the complacent energy that often shows up in mature souls. When a level four soul feels too much pressure to be perfect—not just internally, but also from external sources such as family or culture—that's a sure-fire way to create a slacker personality. When the pressure becomes too great, in the blink of an eye, they can swing from being excited about creating or working on a project, to genuinely not caring.

Like early level-five old souls, mature souls can become *very* frustrated with younger souls. While they see and appreciate differences among people, they can have a hard time with younger souls, because they've been judging themselves for so long, it's natural for them to judge others. Again, it's very important to remember that part of the reason that learning about soul development is so important is so we can start to heal and release that judgment. This is a big challenge for the mature soul—to allow younger souls to do what they are here to do and not try to control them. *It can be tempting to try to "teach" someone out of what they are here to accomplish.* The mature soul is learning how to let others be just who and how they are, while allowing themselves the same grace.

Once they've accepted a younger soul as they really are, they often will want to help them along so much that sometimes they can end up being very pushy, wanting to share what they know, what peace they've found, or anything else that's worked for them. They can be found trying to convince everyone that they've ever met that *their* way is *the* way to have peace, or to have health, or the way to have a better relationship, and on and on. Mature souls must learn to wait for someone to ask for advice. Eventually they'll learn to not take it personally or take offense when others aren't ready for their words of wisdom. This is, of course, easier when you're not related to the person in question.

Where They Are

Mature souls gravitate toward cities. They tend to crave the forward, progressive, more liberal thinking of the city, and some can handle the intensity of that environment on a daily basis. Much like old souls, they can function in the city, but to really thrive, they need hiatus time outside in nature and on the outskirts.

Often, mature souls feel that they're much older souls than they are, and they'll feel that they are in the final stage of incarnation. Does this sound like you, if you're discussing reincarnation? "I never want to do this again, I don't want to come back again, I'm done, this is definitely going to be my last lifetime." If that's your attitude, you can rest assured this is not your last lifetime. I'll explain why as we delve into the old soul realm in the next chapter. For now, just know that you still have some development coming if you're feeling like "earth school" is too challenging and you don't want to come back. More than likely, you will return again, and it'll be your choice to do so, believe it or not. This resistance is a normal phase and a normal feeling. If this resonates with you, then you probably have one foot in the mature soul realm and one in the old soul world. This feeling too, shall pass.

These souls can be politically-minded and peacefully (and sometimes not so peacefully) protest wrongs to try and make changes. They believe so deeply about right and wrong that they push duality on a daily basis. Everything will tend to be labeled good or bad, right or wrong. They are promoters of justice for sure, so if you've been wronged, they'll want to find the perpetrator and make sure they are brought to justice. Mature souls make great judges, lawyers, detectives and advocates for that reason.

These souls can tend to feel victimized easily, especially during the tail end of this phase. Anytime they're not getting what they want, or what they think they deserve, they'll easily feel wronged. The concept that what other people do isn't an assault on them isn't an option for them. When someone like a co-worker, their child, spouse, or friend disagrees with them, it can easily be felt as disrespect, instead of a difference of opinion. It's challenging for the soul in this phase to see that disagreement isn't necessarily disrespect.

Health and the Mind

They tend to read or study a lot, especially books about the heart, the mind, brain development and health. Some of our greatest researchers and scientists are in this soul level. Solving a mystery or getting to the bottom of a problem is a great intellectual motivator for people in this level.

Mature souls eventually seek health on all levels, but there can be blockages to doing what needs to be done to stay well. They will learn what needs to happen, but then have trouble with follow-through, especially in regard to their own health. Over-doing and under-doing are both potential pitfalls in this phase.

The mind of a level four soul is so busy, it's always moving, and that can make things like meditation difficult. These folks were the inspiration for my "Meditation for Busy-Minded People" classes. They can obsess over things, repeating the same or similar thoughts over and over, until it's fully resolved within them. It can really help them when they create something from that busy-mindedness, like writing books, creating art, starting businesses, launching new concepts and ideas. The mind can be their ally, but they need to always be on guard against excesses, since they tend to prioritize "doing" over "being."

The level four soul is still halfway in the "doer" category, while they are moving into the "being" realm. This means that mature souls can accomplish a lot in their lifetimes. One of the differences between level-four and level-three souls is that level-three adolescent souls are doers with a focus on external gratification. The level-four mature souls want to feel good and help others feel good. It's not as much about accumulation.

By the way, being vs. doing doesn't mean that older souls don't ever do anything! It means that the older the soul, the less struggle and hardship is experienced when doing. Older souls tend to do things because it feels right, and if something goes wrong, it doesn't create a lot of stress; it's viewed as an opportunity to find peace in a challenging situation. A mature soul will encounter hardship while doing, and see it either as a reason to get frustrated and quit, or to prove their worth by persevering through hardship. Many times they've equated hard work with value or worth, and they tend to believe that if something is coming easily, it's not worth much.

The lower chakras that were intensified in earlier lifetimes will give you some issues in this level. Mature souls tend toward digestion issues, throat problems, and absorption issues. While any soul age can have those problems, they're more common in level fours because they're learning how to literally "digest" what's happened in their lives and "absorbing" the wisdom so they can move on.

They'll have energy, not as much as level three adolescent souls, but energy to do things for their cause, whatever that is. This could even be the cause of providing for the family. As I mentioned, they can tend toward extremism in diet or exercise, because they are still trying to prove their value or worth through perceived discipline and hard work.

Family and other attachments are huge in this phase, and level fours can tend to feel more obligated than other groups. They'll gravitate toward others in their level and want to socialize and form groups around the concepts of learning, healing and charitable work.

Many charities and rescue organizations are headed and filled with level-four souls. Thank goodness we have a lot of them on the planet at this time! Like every soul age, they are needed and appreciated for the specific gifts they embody. Many of them will work tirelessly for what they believe in, sometimes even acquiring fame for their efforts.

While the heart is the primary focus in this level, the throat chakra is beginning to wake up in a new way to allow for more heart-centered expression. Over time, the need to discuss feelings and share their personal growth with others becomes more important than ever before. Before the throat chakra comes fully into its own (which happens in the old soul phase), the mature soul can tend to fluctuate between dominating the conversation with their newly self-appreciated voice, and shutting down verbally.

The good news is that their conversation is typically well thought out and fully researched, if needed. But can they argue! Many attorneys are mature souls, not just because they tend to be able to hold up their end of a debate, but also because it's common to find them fighting for someone else's rights. Justice is a large aspect of this soul's path. If they feel that there has been an injustice to them or a friend, or even strangers in another country, you will most likely hear about it from someone in this soul phase. One of their beautiful characteristics is that they will also tend to take action to correct that perceived or actual injustice.

In the entire population of the planet right now, about fifteen percent are mature souls. These excellent leaders and helpers can be found many times either learning about or picking up the pieces of faulty systems, businesses, social issues or individuals. Their empathy and courage to stand up for their beliefs makes them so valuable in positions of authority and leadership.

Any and every field imaginable could benefit from having these souls involved, and as long as they feel like they're helping or serving in a meaningful way, they can stick with that task for the long haul. If they're not recognized or appreciated for their contributions, the backlash can be brutal. It's not so much about being seen as the ultimate authority; it's more about just being seen and, as the throat chakra awakens, heard, as well.

Frustration can also rear its head when they feel that someone is being apathetic or not taking enough action to correct something that's obviously wrong (in their perception). If you're seeing yourself in this trait, your challenge is to allow yourself to understand the differences in soul age enough to give younger souls some leeway in the "right action" department. Mature souls can become enraged when younger souls are perceived as self-serving or self-absorbed, or not "awake" enough to help where they could.

Speaking of frustration, it's the older souls that they can really get annoyed with! While on one level they want to learn so much from older souls, they certainly have a hard time understanding why an older soul wouldn't take action to right a wrong that was done "to them." The shift happens when it's understood that an older soul doesn't necessarily feel victimized by the situation. As the energy of the throat and the heart chakras are intensifying during these years, there can be a lot of drama that goes along with that.

> *"The most courageous act is still to think for yourself. Aloud."* ~ Coco Chanel

The spiritual teachers in this level are all about processing through speech and research.

- Speaking your truth.
- Studying your situation through others' experiences.
- Allowing others to learn from your experiences (opening the heart and the throat chakras).

At this level, there is an attempt to balance all of the energy centers, working up to the heart, and the beginnings of work in the throat chakra.

- The Earth Star
- The Root
- Sacral
- Solar Plexus
- Heart
- Throat (just beginning)

The overall growth during mature soul lifetimes will be focused on the issues that originate in the heart chakra, including:

- Lack of understanding of younger and older souls
- Obsessive or compulsive energy
- Feeling suspicious of others; trust issues
- Lack of generosity
- Indifference
- Hiding the heart, withdrawing the emotions
- Perceiving that having emotions is a weakness

The most positive, wonderful aspects of this soul age include:

- Ambition and drive
- Ability to love openly, when balanced
- Motivated to research and learn helpful information
- Incredibly generous with time and energy, when balanced
- Ability to create and sustain deep bonds with others, when in the later stages of this phase
- Charitable and innovative in helpful ways
- Can be very empathetic and caring in the later stages
- Strengthening of the will forces, the ability to "power-through"

If you feel like you're a mature or old soul at this point, and you see yourself in some of these soul traits, you can know that you're working on healing your heart chakra from the wounds that are still unhealed from many previous incarnations. In this lifetime, these wounds then contribute to you having issues or traumas emerge between the ages of 22 and 28, and the ages 71 through age 77.

How do you know if you have unhealed issues from when you were a level four soul that resulted in issues in this lifetime that began during those ages?

- If you have trouble trusting others, even if they've proven their trustworthiness
- If you tend to obsess about problems and have trouble letting go
- If you're holding onto hurt, pain, anger or a grudge
- If you have charitable, generous feelings but have trouble acting on them

- If you experienced abandonment or heartbreak that still hurts or causes you to shut down
- If you are addicted to romance novels
- If you are involved in animal rescue and it's taken over every aspect of your life
- If you regularly find yourself on an emotional roller coaster
- If you fantasize about true love, but have trouble believing that it could exist for you

Here are your tools to help you heal and move forward!

Affirmations

I am open to love and gratitude.

I express myself clearly and easily.

It's safe for me to know myself well.

I see love; I am love.

Centering

Close your eyes and rest your hands in your lap. Sense that there's a small, beautiful budding flower in the center of your chest. As you breathe naturally, allow that flower to begin to blossom further with every breath. It becomes as glorious as any flower you've ever seen. Allow the feeling of this new life, bathed in sunshine, to flood your consciousness. Stay in this energy as long as you like. Anytime you feel unbalanced or in need of the feelings of love or gratitude, return to this centering vision.

Mantra

Yam (sounds like Yahm, elongating the YAAH sound gently into the AHMM)

or

any of the affirmations above

For a free recording of these mantras and other audios that you can listen to and gain the benefits from, even while you sleep, visit our special webpage for readers of this book: alyssamalehorn.com/hoiys

Mudra

Hridaya Mudra

Benefits: Helps to open the heart center, assists in regulating emotions and blood pressure, and helps to relieve anxiety and tension.

Technique: Sit in a comfortable position, and with each hand, roll the index finger into the base of the thumb. Then join the tip of the thumb to the tips of the middle and ring fingers. Extend the little finger. Rest your hands on the tops of your thighs, palms facing up. Hold for 5 to 45 minutes, incorporating a mantra or an affirmation from this chapter if you like, or visualizing a beautiful sunrise or a blossoming flower in the heart area, as in the preceding centering exercise.

(see image on next page)

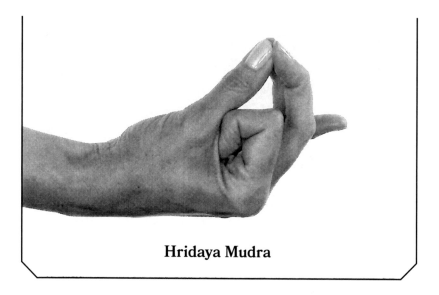

Hridaya Mudra

Guided Meditation

For a free recording of this meditation and other audios that you can listen to and follow along with, visit our special webpage for readers of this book: alyssamalehorn.com/ hoiys

Take a few deep breaths, and start to let the air flow all the way down into your belly. Relax your stomach and your hips, allowing yourself to fully breathe... slowly and gently. As you read this, say "Thank you" to all of your Divine helpers, guides, angels, and the Great Spirit.

Now you're going to invite in the energy that you need for your healing. Just take some deep breaths. This is your time now. You can leave all of your worries behind. Nobody needs anything from you right now. You can just allow yourself to relax into the flow of this moment and just keep breathing. Whatever comes into your mind is just right for you. Any intrusive thoughts that come in while you're doing this... they're supposed to be there. Don't judge them; just let them move through. If you notice any sounds, just acknowledge them and let them go. This time is all for you.

Let your breathing go into a normal, relaxed, rhythmic breath. Now you're going to tell your body to relax. Let your feet and legs soften into the position they're in, relax your hands, allow your shoulders to drop, and allow your body to fully soften down and relax into a natural, comfortable position. Take another deep breath. Now you're going to allow your head and face to relax, your scalp, your forehead, all the tiny muscles around your eyes, your jaw, your muscles around your mouth... just let them all soften and relax. Just take a cleansing breath in and, on your exhale, you're breathing out all of the tension in your body. Now you can allow your breathing to fall into its own natural rhythm again. Don't try to control it in any way; just observe it. You're breathing relaxation in, and you're breathing tension out. If any thoughts flow into your mind, just allow them to flow on past.

I want you to bring your attention to your chest area. Imagine that you have a beautiful green light there in your chest, and it's swirling around like a little whirlpool. Just notice how that feels, how it looks in your mind's eye, and if any thoughts are coming into your mind, think, "That's interesting," and let that thought go.

Focus back on the green light in your chest. As this whirlpool of green light spins in your chest, notice that it starts to gently spread out and get bigger as it spins. It's a beautiful green color. Whatever green color comes to your mind is just the right color. Now draw your attention back to your breath, and as you breathe in, just imagine that you're breathing in more of that green light. It can be emerald, it can be a spring green—whatever color comes to you, you're just breathing that down into your chest area. With every in-breath, you're pulling in more of that green light. It's filling your heart chakra; it's filling your whole chest area. In these next few breaths you're going to let that green light spread out into your whole body. It's going to go down into your arms and hands, down into your torso, into your legs, all the way down into your toes. With every breath you take in, you're breathing more green light... It's coming up into your chest, up into your head, it's connecting with all of your other chakras, and you're just filled with beautiful green light.

Draw your attention back to the chest area, to the center of that green light that's the swirling green area. In the center of that whirlpool, I want you to picture a little pink rosebud. As your attention goes to this pink rose bud, the petals start to unfurl. Petal by petal, it's opening out into a beautiful pink flower that's surrounded by that glowing green light. Your flower may even have a little golden center. Know now that as you are opening your heart center to give and to receive love freely, you are safe. Now you're safe to allow your heart to heal.

As you breathe in this green light, it's bringing you love, compassion, forgiveness, and an open heart. While you're working in that open heart, you're going to neutralize some of the non-beneficial energies that may be residing there, in your heart center. These may be thoughtforms, they may be residue, they may be patterns, anything that you're no longer learning from, you no longer need, that's no longer beneficial—you're going to neutralize those energies now and release them, and then you will replace them consciously with some energies that you choose.

As you continue focusing on that green light and you can still see your pink rosebud (if that's easy for you to visualize), you're going to go ahead and give thanks for all of the energies that are no longer serving you. You're giving thanks and recognizing that they're no longer needed. You're now neutralizing the energies of grief, heartbreak, sadness, bitterness, lack of forgiveness, lack of appropriate boundaries. Take a deep breath, and you'll also neutralize the energy of old injuries or illness, any issues with the heart or back, lungs, breathing issues, breast problems, you'll neutralize all of the energies that are non-beneficial there. Any residue from surgeries, injuries, any residue of feeling left out, you neutralize those as well. You neutralize the energies of isolation and loneliness. You'll neutralize all of those energies. Any other thoughts of non-beneficial issues that come to your mind, you're neutralizing them, as well. Whether it's a lack of peace, the energy of arguments, divorce, fear... you neutralize all of that now. You're deleting and uncreating those energies within you, from this lifetime, from any other lifetime, from all time, space, dimensions and realities.

Say now, silently in your mind, "I allow this healing." With a deep breath, invite in and give thanks for a new upgraded, fresh set of energies to fill that heart center. Invite in and give thanks for the energies of love, compassion, generosity, wellness and vitality, inclusion, partnership, healing, confidence, stable blood pressure, good circulation, forgiveness, lightness of being and light-heartedness, good humor, and fun. Invite in and give thanks for the energy of freedom, as your soul remembers that as its natural state. The energy of joy, harmony, balance, resolution, peace, and any other positive energies that come to your mind now, go ahead and invite them in; you're giving thanks for them now.

You're now creating healing from all of your lifetimes as a fourth level mature soul and as an adult in this lifetime (even if you're a young person now). Affirm: "I allow all appropriate, optimal, beneficial, and benevolent healing from all of my lifetimes as a mature soul, and in this lifetime, from the moment that I became 22 years old until my final moment of age 28. I allow all of the appropriate, optimal, beneficial, and benevolent healing."

Focus on your breath. In your mind, silently say, "I allow this healing. I allow love, compassion, forgiveness. I allow all fear to be completely dissolved." Now focus your attention on your heart and feel that wonderful green glow, as it's still gently spinning in that chest area. With your next breath, you're breathing in that green light, and you're breathing out tension. Now say in your mind, "I am loving, I am loveable, I am loved." Now visualize that swirling green light that encompassed your body. Visualize it getting smaller and smaller in your chest, until it's the perfect size for you. It's perfectly balanced; it's perfectly harmonized. Whatever size it ends up becoming, it's perfect for you. You're pulling it up from your legs, you're pulling it all back down from your crown, pulling it back into your heart until it's whatever size that is perfectly balanced and harmonious for you.

Say to yourself three times, "My heart chakra is perfectly balanced and harmonized. My heart chakra is perfectly balanced and harmonized. My heart chakra is perfectly balanced and harmonized." Now take a deep breath, and let it out slowly. Whenever you're ready, you can kind of move your shoulders a little bit, start to be more aware of the room around you, and open your eyes.

At this point, you now have a fully awakened, beautifully balanced, root, sacral, solar plexus and heart chakra system. All of your other chakras are beginning their realignment and recalibration process in preparation for the next chapters. You may do this exercise as often as you like, especially when you feel lacking in love, gratitude or understanding.

"When you're an older soul, you're given the opportunity to heal yourself on every level, and in so many ways."

~ CHAPTER 7 ~

OLD SOULS

"If everyone demanded peace instead of another television set, then there'd be peace."
~ John Lennon

LET'S GET A COMMON MISCONCEPTION about old souls out of the way. Some people believe that old souls are peaceful and loving all the time, like a wise, patient monk, and that they never get angry or upset. That they have a mystical "knowing" as they gently nod and size up every situation in their lives. There's some truth to this idea, as old souls near the end of this phase, but typically, the earlier lifetimes in the old soul phase are pretty far from peaceful!

The beginning of this soul phase can actually be pretty rough. Regardless of where old souls are within the phase, whether they've just moved into the old soul realm or they're on the tail end, they are far more sensitive than the souls around them, typically even the family they are brought up in. This can lead to feelings of isolation and frustration. Many can struggle with addiction and low self-esteem, the results of feeling out of place for so long. There's a world-weariness that also rears its head in the early parts of this phase; it's typically marked by the phrase, "This *has* to be my last lifetime, I'm never doing this again!" as I mentioned earlier. If this sounds like you, this definitely isn't your last lifetime.

You know you're moving into the last lifetimes—the finale—when you're so overwhelmed with the energy of love, there's literally nothing to complain about. The magic and mystery of life, the beauty of the earth, the experiences in your world—all become more reasons to naturally and easily feel grateful and at peace. Stress doesn't play a starring role when you're in your final lifetime. You're not buying into the illusion of this life. You have truly integrated the understanding that everything is an exercise to help you grow and develop on a soul level. Regardless of your current soul age, this chapter will help you understand yourself better, help you lose your anxiety, be prepared for what's to come, and move through your life with more happiness and enthusiasm.

The overall chakra focus of the old soul includes all of the main seven chakras.

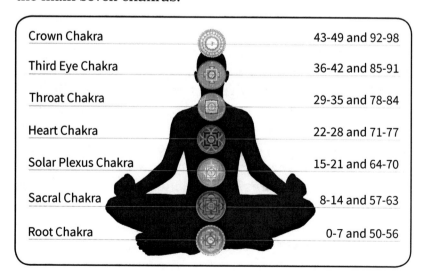

Crown Chakra	43-49 and 92-98
Third Eye Chakra	36-42 and 85-91
Throat Chakra	29-35 and 78-84
Heart Chakra	22-28 and 71-77
Solar Plexus Chakra	15-21 and 64-70
Sacral Chakra	8-14 and 57-63
Root Chakra	0-7 and 50-56

Even with every chakra activated in the old soul's journey, there's a dramatic emphasis on the throat, brow and crown chakras. The most active chakra development and healing is during these physical ages:

43–49 and 92–98:   Crown (Connection with Spirit)

36–42 and 85–91:   Third Eye/Brow (Intuition & Knowing)

29–35 and 78–84:   Throat (Expression)

While on the one hand, this means that the old soul has had more experience working with these energy centers and has the opportunity to move through healing more efficiently, it also means that old souls have experienced so many previous lifetimes, there can be deep wounds in every chakra, and they can fall into any of the more painful patterns of any and every soul age.

Remember, if you're identifying with the old soul phase, but still notice some traits within you that seem to be younger soul traits, that's a normal, unavoidable part of the process. As you're moving through the sub-levels within the old soul level, you're healing and releasing the residue of wounds from other, earlier ages.

> The throat chakra is the center of personal expression. We develop this chakra during our old soul lifetimes and, in this current lifetime, between the ages of 29 and 35, and again between the ages of 78 and 84. As the throat chakra develops and heals, we learn how to express ourselves clearly

and without fear of repercussions. When this chakra is in need of healing, issues surface in every aspect of communication, including self-talk. If you feel repressed verbally or feel that what you say isn't important, if you swallow your words, if you engage in expressing criticism (whether toward others or yourself), then it's time to clear your throat chakra. Use the tools at the end of this chapter to begin the process.

Expression

Old souls tend to have more trouble with expression than other soul ages. This is due to their desire to have emotional and spiritual clarity and, at the same time feeling afraid to hurt others. The healthy, balanced energy of the throat chakra makes it possible to express ourselves fully and clearly, without fear. But it's during this fifth level of soul development that the throat chakra is becoming fully activated. You'll know this is happening when you have one dialogue expressing silently in your mind, and a different dialogue coming out of your mouth. For this reason, the opening of the throat chakra can be hard on relationships. Ultimately, the goal is to have the strength and willingness to speak your truth in a kind way, without being afraid of experiencing some form of punishment or backlash for expressing yourself.

Some old souls have the opposite issue, where they tend to over-speak or are tactless. This is also a throat chakra imbalance, in that it's too open, too expansive and not in harmony with the other chakras. It's a result of a deep fear of being hurt or not being loved. Balancing the throat chakra is often the most noticeable of all energy healing, because the results are almost immediate. The tools at the end of this chapter will help you clear up any issues in that area, so that you can feel free to express yourself in the best way possible for you.

The Significance of Old Souls

It's important to remember that a second grader isn't being defiant if they're not able to do college-level work. They're going to do what makes sense to them and what they need to do to grow and learn. It also doesn't make the college student better than the second grader. It just means that they have more development and experience behind them. This is the bottom line of soul age and one of the most important things to remember. Soul age is not an indicator of superiority or inferiority. It's a gauge for compassionate understanding of ourselves and others. When the ego gets involved and you feel more important or better than another, whether you're using the criteria of soul age (or gender or race or physical age or...), you know that you're not perceiving reality accurately, and you're allowing your fear of not being good enough to direct your feelings (the mind's favorite trick).

We tend to respect and honor old souls because we can feel that they're holding wisdom, love and a balanced energy that younger souls haven't yet developed, much like how we will honor and respect our elders in our physical community. However, respect and honor aren't based on whether someone is a better person. We tend to honor the old soul's experiences and how they've translated those into a refinement of their authentic selves. Very old souls tend to become spiritual teachers, and that also can inspire respect and appreciation, but we can also find spiritual teachers in every soul age, to support those moving through that phase.

Beliefs

Is it easier to be an old soul than a young soul? Most old souls would probably laugh at that assumption! Many feel that it's much more challenging. The primary difficulty comes from three issues: first, the release of fixed beliefs. Secondly, the onset of more open, vague beliefs, and third, confusion about identity and sense of self during the growth and development of those new beliefs.

It's much easier to believe whatever your parents taught you or to believe what everyone in your church or culture believes. When you're an old soul, you reach a point of questioning everything you've bought into. Younger souls tend to skip this step, and adolescent souls tend to rebel against whatever they were taught without deeply exploring why. This questioning can bring some old souls into depression and anxiety, because it's not just the inner conflict of "What do I really believe?"; it also comes with the feelings of not belonging and fear of exclusion and disconnection.

Younger souls tend to feel like they belong, as long as there are shared beliefs or goals. Old souls can still feel isolated, sometimes even in a group of other old souls, regardless of shared beliefs or goals. All of the issues that plague the other soul phases can affect the old soul. This is the only soul group that is dealing with unhealed aspects of every one of the previous soul phases—and that's a lot to cope with! Lots of old wounding and outdated patterns will come up in the old soul's life, for them to decide whether or not they're ready to see reality in a new and more accurate light.

Sensitivity

It's generally true that old souls are more sensitive. When an old soul is a child, they will tend to be sensitive to noise, violence, sarcasm—basically anything that doesn't fall under the headings of peace, acceptance and love. Since parents aren't perfect, this leaves old souls struggling to understand where they stand in the family, how they fit into the world. All souls struggle with this, regardless of soul age, but older souls internalize the struggle in a deeper way. There can be a tendency toward hopelessness if they don't get the support they need at some point in their development.

The type of support that best serves the old soul is gentle acceptance, with some direction toward self-love. This can come from parents, teachers, friends, even a book. For me, my parents were very accepting of me, even when they didn't understand me. They allowed me to express myself, but I still wasn't secure enough in what I was feeling as a child to be as open as I could've been. When I was an older teen and young adult, I read books about different religions and cultures that helped me open up significantly. Just learning that there were others in the world who had beliefs that differed from my own upbringing helped me to open, to see how I was really relating to the world through the lens of my beliefs.

Many old souls will be sensitive to foods, the environment, alcohol, sugar, and just about anything you could regard as toxic. The older the soul, the more finely tuned the nervous system can be. Many years ago, I was complaining to my doctor about how sensitive I was to perfumes, gasoline fumes, gluten, cigarette smoke, and on and on. I felt like the princess and the pea. He told me something that changed my life. He said that people like me had "Maserati neurology" and that no one ever complained about a spark plug needing a slight adjustment on such a finely tuned machine as a Maserati. I realized that being "finely tuned" was a gift and it contributed to me being so naturally skilled in my work as a spiritual teacher, psychic medium and healer.

This shift in perception actually helped my sensitivity symptoms dramatically. I was contributing to a weakened condition with my critical thoughts about the way that I was. When I shifted into immense gratitude for the way I naturally am, my body, mind, soul and spirit worked together much more smoothly, with fewer reactions to chemicals and toxins. It was a long, complex journey to heal from such intense chemical sensitivity, but that was a turning point that changed my trajectory. Note that I was willing to release my frustration and replace it with gratitude. I was open to shifting out of an out-worn mode into a fresh, new way of thinking. Having an open mind toward these shifts is critical at this stage.

"I am losing precious days. I am degenerating into a machine for making money. I am learning nothing in this trivial world of men. I must break away and get out into the mountains to learn the news." ~ John Muir

How to Be In the Mix

Chaos and crowds can be like kryptonite for old souls, especially as they move into the later stages of this soul age. The reasons that you might feel either hyped up and unstable or exhausted and drained by crowds are all based in energy. There are thousands, if not millions, of thoughtforms in a group of only a hundred people. Those thoughtforms are energy bodies that have a quality of frequency that's in alignment with the original thought. If you're in a group of a hundred people, how many thoughtforms of jealousy do you think are floating around? What about unworthiness? Or hurried energy? This is a lot to feel, to process, or to try to block out!

For an old soul to be happy in life, we must learn how to filter out any energies that aren't positive or uplifting for us, instead of habitually taking in everything that happens very deeply. By nature, old souls want to help and serve others, and one of the ways we do that is by attempting to digest and metabolize the negative energy that is plaguing others, many times without even realizing we're doing it. This is not only exhausting and not good for us in any way, but it also steps on other people's lessons and attempts to control their experience by healing it for them, instead of helping them in an upgraded way. It's the proverbial difference between "teaching someone to fish" and just giving them dinner.

What an act of love it is to stay in our own centeredness and peace, and to allow others to feel their feelings without trying to purify them, without them (or us) even consciously realizing it! Old souls are so sensitive to other people's feelings that, many times, we will be the peacemakers in family or work situations, and we'll do *anything* that's needed for everyone else to feel okay and be okay. There's a selfish motivation lurking under the surface in this dynamic. We are so empathic and feel other people's feelings so deeply, we need them to feel okay so we can feel okay. This can become a habitual way of relating that stems from childhood. Did you try to be perfect (to make sure mom or dad was okay with your behavior), or think that you were taking care of or protecting your parents from stress? Even into adulthood, some old souls carry this pattern of feeling like we have to monitor other people's "contentment quotient," and make any necessary adjustments to try to improve their happiness level.

Once this pattern is ingrained, what happens when we enter that crowd of a hundred people we talked about? We unconsciously act out the pattern, even when we're with scores of people we don't even know. Even if we don't ever speak to those people! It's like our energy field is acting as the emotional janitor for other people's stuff. For old souls, this can be the most draining aspect of being in large groups.

What if we revamped and upgraded our way of being with other people, and just allowed them to feel however they need to feel, in order for them to learn their own lessons? They could use the exercises in life that have been provided for them to facilitate their own soul's growth, and you could be supportive and positive, but not take it on for them. What a gift we give our loved ones when we allow them the same opportunities that we are becoming more conscious of and learning how to accept! Every challenge allows us a chance to flex those soul muscles, and who are we to take that workout away from our spiritually out-of-shape family members? We're all coming from a place of being out-of-shape spiritually, and we all have our own work to do!

As I was healing my own habit of taking on other people's feelings, one of the phrases that has come to me in meditation is that the pattern is "beautifully intentioned, and completely inappropriate." I love that way of looking at it, because we can know that the intention is for us to feel better and for our loved ones to feel better—and yes, that is beautiful! It is also totally inappropriate for us to ever try to "make" someone feel better. Trying to control other people's thoughts, feelings or reality is never appropriate. We each have to choose to feel good and happy. We can choose to be supportive and encouraging and loving, and when you identify what is your cross to bear and what isn't, you're well on your way to authenticity.

The most miraculous aspect of this new way of being is that—when you embrace this pattern of seeking your own contentment and you're willing to release control of other people's emotional condition—on its own, your presence will actually start to shift the environment and the people around you! The peace and harmony you were aiming for all along can be achieved through just focusing on awakening those energies within yourself, and by osmosis, others will pick up on that energy and start to emulate it, as well. You're creating a template for others to follow, and what a gift that is. There's another potential outcome, if they're not ready to feel better and they're still learning from their angst. When that's the case, they'll go somewhere else, far away from you. Either way, all is well.

Are You a Control Freak?

The controlling energy of the old soul is less about wanting to make sure everyone does what the old soul thinks they should do; it's more about wanting to make sure that everyone makes decisions that would result in that other person having peace of mind. Why is this so important? Because the older soul is so empathic, they tend to feel everyone's feelings, and if someone else feels bad or sad, it actually is painful for the old soul. The control is because "If you feel bad, and I'm connected in with you, then I feel bad." The controlling energy is based in a feeling that if I can't control how *you* feel, then I can't control how *I* feel. Use the tools at the end of this chapter to help you release control and embrace freedom! You'll also see a simple and easy way to strengthen your energy field, so that crowds are less draining.

Children

Record numbers of those coming into the world now are old souls. These children have had many, many lifetimes and you can see the wisdom and experience in their eyes. These are the kids who are the most psychic, and you'll know this because they'll tell you what they're seeing and feeling in the spirit world. They typically have a great way of expressing themselves, even from a young age.

This applies primarily to old souls who were born from about 1990 to the present day. These kids have a keener sense of their spiritual mission from a much earlier age, although this doesn't mean to imply that they'll easily find their career; that's a different ball of wax we'll cover later in this chapter. Spiritually, they don't have to wait until they're 35 or 40 years old to be able to access the wisdom and evolution that they are bringing from their many earlier lifetimes. They also will tend to challenge their parents by not conforming to whatever the standard expectations are. They are often described as having a sweet innocence, even if they're in their teen years and acting out inappropriately. You can still sense the age of the soul and the innate "spiritual connection" energy in them.

The ones who remember their psychic abilities when they are born will tend to talk about it and not hide what they're feeling. They're not afraid to tell you that there's a "man standing over there" or that they see "shadow people" or that they heard a voice, but no one was there.

It's so important to validate the experiences of these kids, even if you don't understand what's going on, even if you're frightened, even if you don't see what they see. All of us feel loved when we feel validated and understood, and none of us feel safe when someone tells us that it's our imagination or a dream, and to just forget whatever is scaring us. If your child seems to be an older soul than you are, use the opportunity to hone your empathy, put yourself in their shoes and help them feel safe.

Speaking of empathy, the other quality of old souls that comes through when we're children is the extremely high level of empathy connected to the feeling of trying to constantly make everyone around us feel better. We will be absorbed with the energy of everyone around us, and not know how we really feel. As we get older, it takes a lot of practice to separate those feelings out and have some clarity about our own emotions, and at the same time let other people have whatever feeling they are going to have.

If you're an old soul and had some of these experiences as a child, it's important to heal any issues you may still be carrying of not feeling validated or understood. I can promise you that every parent does the very best they can, with whatever level of soul development they are currently in and in whatever frequency they are currently resonating. However, even if you truly believe that, sometimes there are issues that are still unresolved and need to be healed for you to move forward with the feelings of freedom and liberation.

The patterns from childhood were all you knew at that time, and as you develop in the physical world, you're developing spiritually, as well. In this process, every little discomfort or old hurt will begin rise to the surface to be healed. This doesn't mean that we have to involve our parents or siblings in our healing, even if they are part of the wounding. It means that the hurt and pain is there, and once it's recognized, we have a responsibility to bring light to the darkness (healing to the wound).

The brow chakra (also called the third-eye chakra) is the home of our intuition, our spiritual sight. We develop this chakra during our old soul lifetimes, and in this current lifetime between the ages of 36 and 42 and again between the ages of 85 and 91. When the brow chakra is activated, open and clear, we can intuitively see and know the deeper meanings and truths in all situations. We can move beyond the role of victim or "challenged one," into the observer or witness position. Observing our own thoughts and patterns with the gentle third eye enables us to shift out of cultural expectations into our own chosen reality. If you find yourself unable to detach from your issues, fears and confusion, you know it's time to activate and heal the brow chakra. Open up to intuitive clarity by using the tools at the end of this chapter.

"Today you are You, that is truer than true.
There is no one alive who is Youer than You."
~ Dr. Suess

Choosing Our Parents

Old souls can have childhood experiences that are just as challenging as other soul ages. Sometimes the challenge is centered around home life; sometimes it's a childhood illness, learning difficulties, or other things. You may recall from earlier chapters that I talked about how we choose our parents, our geographic location, our intelligence level, our physical looks, and how we'll learn the soul lessons that we've set up for ourselves for each individual lifetime. As we develop on a soul level, the motivations for those choices change. During the life between lives, a younger soul will choose their parents based on what those parents can offer them: good genes, a specific life experience, a chance to be wealthy from birth, the perceived safety of a tribal community, or the lack of pressure to change (a community very rooted in rigid tradition).

One of the hallmarks of an old soul is the motivation behind the choosing of their parents. An old soul chooses their parents with one powerful thought: "I know what they need!" Then it gets followed up with something like, "I could bring empathy; they look like they could really use that," or "One of them is an alcoholic. I bet they really need a stable, centered energy; I'll bring that," and so on. There is usually at least one old soul in every family. That soul helps to keep the energy stable, even if that person chooses to detach from the family at some point. Old souls will sometimes disconnect from the family if it's too dysfunctional and painful to be connected; at other times, younger souls will disconnect from a family because the old soul energy is too overwhelming.

When an old soul is a child in human form and dealing with the complexities of family life, that soul may tend to feel responsible for their parents' happiness or wellness. This may carry over into an "inappropriate guilt" cycle, even through adulthood. This is illustrated when an adult child is still trying to make sure that his or her parents are feeling okay and loved, even if the parents are perhaps abusive or not open to the love from the adult child.

This paragraph may contain the most important truth for every old soul to hear, so pay attention, old souls! When we elect to come here, to have this incarnation with these parents and these looks and this kind of intelligence, and we choose to bring a gift to our family, like the gift of empathy or sensitivity or stability, *how that gift is received is not our business.*

This is a huge revelation for most old souls. So what is your business? As we grow older, it's our responsibility to continue to allow self-love to grow and transmit our gifts with the highest intention we can muster. We can educate ourselves about the common old soul issues: codependency; inappropriate guilt; how we brought empathy or unconditional love to the family, for example, and how to leave it at that. Instead of *managing* our expectations, how liberating it is to completely relieve yourself of expectations altogether! In this stage of development, you don't need specific *results* from your actions—you just need to try to be clear with your intentions.

Also, your business is to identify the gift or gifts that are inherent to you, give thanks that you had the opportunity to bring them, and then detach from the outcome. Sometimes this means we must distance ourselves from those family members who are consistently undermining our own growth. If you're not able to keep yourself healthy and well while staying connected to your family, it's completely appropriate to do whatever you need to do to honor and respect yourself. Getting professional emotional or spiritual counseling is key if you find yourself in this situation.

Before you were born, you actually knew how this would most likely play out. Like any other soul age, old souls are in no way obligated to be the object of abuse in an effort to keep the peace. The opposite is actually true. Old souls are obligated to activate the energy of personal responsibility, and in doing so, are encouraged to make decisions based on what is healthiest and most beneficial for themselves. *What is in your highest good is actually in everyone else's highest good around you.* There are no exceptions to this rule! During a time of high emotion, it may not be obvious how that statement could be true. You may feel guilty for ending an abusive relationship or your folks may claim that you're abandoning them, but you can rest assured that, if it's in your highest good to remain close to them or keep your distance, your actions will benefit everyone involved. The truth of that statement will become more and more obvious over time.

~ ~ ~

How you are received is *not* your business.

Setting a positive intention for yourself *is* your business.

How you transmit your energy *is* your business.

Detach from the outcome.

What is in your highest good is in everyone else's highest good too, every time, no matter what.

Affirmation: I am sovereign, I am free.

Relationships

Why would two people of different soul ages ever be attracted to each other? Why would an old soul ever be attracted to or marry a younger soul? There are three main reasons. First, the older soul is trying to heal the younger soul. The empathy from the old soul is attractive to the younger one, and the wounds are so evident in the younger one, the old soul feels compelled to help them along.

Another reason is that old souls tend to see the divine spirit in all people and mistake it for their soul. Let's say you meet someone. You connect. You feel a soul connection, a magnetism; you feel that you've known each other forever, maybe even feel like soul mates. You feel like you're seeing into the other person's soul and you feel that no matter what, you see the vulnerability, the unconditional love, the true nature of the person. Then, let's say they turn on you. You're no longer feeling great about the relationship; they become manipulative or verbally abusive, for example.

This only happens in relationships where one party is a younger soul. The old soul is seeing the *divine spirit* in the other person—the part that is perfect, that every living thing experiences as perfection—not their soul. The old soul many times thinks that they're seeing the other person's soul, but they're actually seeing the beautiful perfection and innocence of their spirit. Every person's soul is carrying around lifetimes of old wounds and patterns that want to be cleared and eventually will be. The soul is bringing the baggage and the desire to purify itself through experiencing the illusion of this life. Even the worst criminals in history have a beautiful, pristine spirit, but the soul of that person may be very young and uninformed about living in the light.

The third reason is much like the reason that physically older people can be attracted to physically younger folks. Old souls are working on healing themselves at a very deep level. The passion of the child soul or the confidence and vitality of the adolescent soul can be incredible magnets for the old soul, as the old soul is working on remembering those aspects of themselves. This is especially true if the old soul is in the early stages of this fifth soul level, when some world-weariness can rear its head. If you're healing something from the time when you were a younger soul, you'll have issues in this lifetime to remind you of what's unhealed, and as you heal, those wounds will draw you to younger souls.

For example, if an old soul has unhealed trauma from their lifetimes as a level-one infant or a level-two child soul, then the old soul will create/allow a sexual trauma in their current life, to draw attention to what's not yet resolved on a soul level. The old soul will be attracted to someone who holds a majority of root chakra or sacral chakra energy (a level one or two soul). If the old soul does their work to heal their own life, using whatever tools appeal to them—psychological counseling, journaling, spirituality, energy healing, yoga—then at some point, they will no longer need to be with the younger soul to help them heal.

The younger soul also benefits tremendously from this pairing, because the old soul's healing creates a pathway or a template for the younger soul to follow, energetically. These types of relationships are 100% mutually beneficial, soul-wise. What a gift we give to each other by engaging in the energy of love, so far beyond just feeling good. If more people understood the nature of attraction from a soul perspective, how much drama could be avoided! When everyone is willing to see the higher level truth behind the connection, gratitude takes the place of resentment.

There's a huge amount of energy required when we address our old wounds through relationships, for both parties. When this becomes exhausting (emotionally or physically), one or both of the souls will feel that it's time for the relationship to complete. Note that I didn't use the word "fail," because relationships are a success in the spiritual world if you're open to the lessons they provide. The concept of relationships failing is not a spiritual concept. We complete our work with those we love, and we may then choose to move on. If we haven't completed the healing, then we will be attracted to and drawn into relationships much like the one we just left. Sometimes we require more than one teacher to really integrate the concepts that we're working on healing.

> "A thousand candles can be lighted from the flame of one candle, and the life of the candle will not be shortened. Happiness can be spread without diminishing that of yourself."
> ~ Mahatma Gandhi

These moments fall under the heading of we talked about before: "What's in my highest good is also in every other human being's highest good, no matter what; no exceptions." One of the souls in these relationships will typically have a difficult time seeing that a split would be best for both people, but there's always one partner who knows deeply that they can no longer be healthy and stay in the relationship. Sometimes the younger soul wants to complete the relationship because they no longer feel connected to the faster growing old soul. Regardless of who wants the ending, relationships get to a point of not being sustainable when the two souls are no longer communicating on a level of mutual soul healing, and exhaustion becomes paramount.

If you are an old soul in a relationship with a younger soul, remember that it's not your job to change anyone. At some point, you were also a younger soul. There are many relationships between people of different soul ages that are working out well, where each person has their role. There are also a lot of divorces happening these days, as people seek freedom from stressful situations that are inhibiting their growth.

You can't force more light into anyone's system and you can't control someone else's development, even though you may think you want to! All you can do is allow more light into your own life, clean up your own side of the street, and any soul that is desiring forward movement can use that energy to help them on their own journey.

The crown chakra is our connection to spirit. We develop this chakra during our old soul lifetimes, and in this current lifetime, between the ages of 43 and 49 and (if we live long enough) again between the ages of 92 and 98. As the crown chakra develops and heals, we see clearly the interconnectedness of all life. We transcend the fear and anxiety that anchors the ego, as we allow the lightness of spirit to be revealed. Gratitude, joy and trust become the norm when this chakra is clear, open and strong. If you are unable to trust yourself (your inner guru), the Creator, or the process of life, it's time to activate and heal the crown chakra. Use the tools at the end of this chapter to begin the process.

"My religion is very simple. My religion is kindness." ~ Dalai Lama XIV

Love Is My Religion

Are you in the sub-phase of being an old soul where organized religion isn't working for you? Being part of an organized religion is rare for old souls, once you've passed a specific growth point. If you're in the later stages of level five, you may tend to outgrow religion and dogma by the time you're physically in your 40s or 50s.

The religion aspect of this old soul phenomenon is pretty simple. When we're in the younger phases of our incarnations, or we're in the early phases of being an old soul, some of us crave structure and ritual within our spiritual lives. We accept the rigidity of the dogma and feel that it's bringing us closer to Source and closer to ourselves on a soul level.

Eventually, as we get closer and closer to that authentic self—the true soul—organized religion starts to feel confining. This is especially true if the dogma of the religion has any exclusivity in it at all, or teaches that everyone must believe the same way to get to heaven or be saved. Eventually, every old soul gets to the point where they know that this isn't the highest truth for them. To some people, it can appear that you're doing a 180 with your beliefs. What's really happening is a distillation and purification of the higher-level meaning behind the religion. In most faiths, the higher-level belief is "Love one another." Once an old soul has completely integrated this simple truth and realized that there are no exceptions to it, any religion or group that attempts to guide someone to think or behave in a particular way (so that they will be worthy of God's love) falls by the wayside.

This simple truth of "love one another" also applies to ourselves, which is the final frontier for most souls. When we're first working with the "love one another" truth and it's still just a concept—not yet an integrated part of us—we also hold other concepts and beliefs that qualify the love. For example, if someone "deserves it": if *I* deserve it, then of course I can love myself. The argument then presents itself in the unhealed parts of the mind: *"How can I truly deserve unconditional love as long as I still remember that really stupid thing I did in 1989 or those times I lost my temper or stayed in a relationship that wasn't good for me? I reserve the right to hold some critical thoughts about myself, thank you very much! You would criticize me, too, if you knew everything about me, saw the drunken nights, heard my inner talk, etc."* You're about to see why I call the self-love phase the final frontier, because all of this changes when you fall in love.

Falling In Love

> *"You know you're in love when you can't fall asleep because reality is finally better than your dreams."* ~ Dr. Seuss

You know that feeling of falling in love? There's a point in every old soul's life where that feeling (including the butterflies, the wonderful peace, enthusiasm and sense of positive expectation) starts to happen, but it's not falling in love with someone else. You're falling in love with yourself, as you start to sense who you really are, on a soul level. As you're reading this, you're receiving some energetic upgrades that are helping you either break into this new realm or deepen this experience.

The soul of you is lovable in every way, and when you begin to connect with yourself on that level, you literally can't help but start to fall in love! When this happens, you have unlocked and started to open the door to real self-love. It can be grand or it can be subtle, but either way, when it happens, your life changes and it will never be the same again.

What you experience in this level is wondrous and exciting. You free up all of that emotional energy that was holding you in the energy of self-criticism and perfectionism. That took a lot of energy to hold those patterns in place, and now you have access to all of that energy! You will notice that you'll naturally use that energy to heal, whether it's a physical issue that's needed to be addressed or an emotional issue that you're ready to complete. This process also includes a revamping of the self-talk that goes on inside your head.

When we have integrated this self-love, this highest level truth of "love one another, and oh yeah, that includes me," it's impossible to hold onto the opposing belief, which is that humans can be right or wrong, good or bad. At the end of this chapter, you'll see some techniques to release those old beliefs and criticisms of ourselves and begin to fully embrace self-love.

Many times this can lead to a vegetarian or vegan lifestyle. There are more vegans in this soul realm than any other. This is a normal, natural progression for old souls— to eventually come to a decision about the way they personally take responsibility for their relationship with the animal kingdom. This doesn't mean every old soul is vegan; it means that eventually, as your soul progresses, you'll be led to adopt an eating regimen that serves you on every level, not just physical nourishment. Be open to what feels right for you, not what you've been told. There is innate wisdom in your feelings and it's safe to explore them, even if you don't have the support of those around you.

Hey, Come Join Us!

The phrase, "Want to join us?" can be a nightmare for some old souls. Depending on where you are in the level five phase, you might feel like running away when someone ask you to join their group, club or order. The main reason for old souls not feeling drawn to join groups or religions, or generally just not feeling like a "joiner," is based in the concept of group karma.

When we join a group, we spiritually agree to take on any and all group karma associated with that organization or group. It's the same concept as family karma, except that, when it comes to groups, we have a conscious choice after we incarnate, as opposed to making the decision to join a family before we're born. Either way, it's a conscious decision; the difference is when and where the decision is made, whether during this lifetime, or before.

Group karma includes issues like greed, power struggles, insecurity, feelings of lack, unworthiness, etc. When those issues have been in the group in the past, or in the lineage of the group, or in the larger corporate religious structure or foundation of the group, most old souls can feel that energy from a mile away and won't join.

You may not know consciously why you don't want to join in, and especially why you don't want to commit to a group, but group karma is usually the reason. Have you ever wondered what that said about you—when everything on paper looks great, you like the people, you believe in the ideals, but for some reason you still just can't commit? It's an effort to be more efficient in this lifetime, and not take on any other projects (karma) that you would have to clear up, somewhere later down the line. That would take time and energy. When you're an old soul, you're in the business of conserving both of those things.

Another side effect of the group issue is the loneliness trait that so many old souls carry. Some even feel it from their earliest memories—feelings of not fitting in at school, or at home—and some gravitate toward adults instead of other kids. This is pretty common for this stage in soul development, not that it makes it easier. When you start to recognize other souls in your soul family, and those that are in the same phase that you are, you'll start to build kind of a "friend family" that many times may not include members of your actual family.

Feeling detached or feelings of not being part of your biological or adoptive family also seem to follow the old soul. This can be better understood if you can determine what soul age your family members are. When you know the phase that they're in, you'll expect them to think, feel and act in alignment with their soul's age, and you won't expect them to behave as if they're older souls than they are. This leads to the ability to suspend judgment and criticism, and overcome feelings of victimization or frustration.

Your Role Is Not Your Soul

Most of us have several roles that we're playing in this lifetime. Part of what makes the old soul's journey so scary is that they're leaving the safety and security of these roles. For example, when you're in the role of "daughter" you can look to your parents and follow their guidance when you're making decisions and choosing how to live your life.

When you are bouncing from role to role in your life, from the role of mom or dad, to wife, to sibling, to son or daughter, to accountant (or whatever your job is), to counselor for your friends, and on and on... it's exhausting! Each role has its own structure that you're fitting into while you're playing that part. It can be reassuring and comforting to have the structure of the role, so you know what's expected of you, you know what to do, and how to regard yourself. Another challenge with this dynamic is that you're identifying with each role and, therefore, you play the part while forgetting who you really are during that time.

The way to transcend the roles and the overwhelm that comes from them is to connect deeply with yourself on a soul level and a heart level. You can simplify your role in this life easily, by consciously choosing only one role—the role of intending love, radiating love—to others, to self, to the planet, to God. Just love. Consider whether you'd like to drop the multi-tasking job descriptions and trade them in for one job—to be love.

Society And Culture

As old souls move into the later stages of the fifth level, they eventually tire of society's way of relating. This includes the literal insanity of the 24-hour news cycle, violent TV shows and movies, sex for the sake of having sex, watching dramatized surgery and crime shows, gossip, and generally anything that you would want to avoid in real life.

Can you imagine being an alien from another planet? You land on Earth, and you want to see what Earthlings do for entertainment. You turn on a television, and you see dramatic representations of the worst and most painful things that could happen to a human. You see actors playing out a human's scariest fears... children being abducted, life or death hospital scenes, crime scene investigations. Then you see reality TV... humans fighting with each other, competing, disrespecting themselves and the people they supposedly love. Then come the paranormal shows, where ghosts (earthbound spirits) are bullied, and psychic children are put in terrifying situations. If you were that alien from another planet, you would have every reason to believe that human beings were determined to feel victimized, overwhelmed, and just generally low vibration—and that they were using television and movies to make sure that these goals were met!

What many people find entertaining is disturbing to an old soul. The above-mentioned energies that are prevalent in our society are not good or bad. These energies either resonate with you or they don't. They are either promoting your well-being or creating more dimension to what you're healing. They're matching your current vibration— matching the vibration you're growing out of or matching what you're shifting into.

Don't be fooled, though. Anyone—old soul or not—can be sucked into the current societal landscape, based on what's ready to be healed within them. For example, if you have any unhealed root chakra issues at all, then you're resonating with the energy of being in survival-mode. You'll be drawn to the surgery shows, crime shows, ghost shows, anything that has life or death as a component. Then you know that it's time to heal from when you were in the first level of soul development, when you were an infant soul.

As another example, if you have unhealed sacral chakra issues, you'll be attracted to the upset and discord that's prevalent in reality TV, where families or neighbors are arguing or generally not expressing the best version of themselves. In this case, you're resonating with the energy of exclusion, not belonging, or not knowing how to feel safe. You also are probably carrying around the fear of not being seen as "right," and scared to be vulnerable.

The challenge is that when you watch something that is in alignment with a part of you that's wounded or not in its highest form, then you proliferate the energy of the wound and it becomes more deeply ingrained within you.

It becomes more challenging to overcome what's wanting to be resolved. The desire to be connected with energy that reminds us of what needs to be healed is normal. However, the healing can only come when we allow ourselves to rise above the wound, see it clearly, and allow it to complete.

Old souls realize that when you watch those things, you are bringing that energy into your life, that it lowers your frequency, and that no progress comes from that. When a level five soul gets overwhelmed, they can easily fall into a phase of watching those types of things, in an effort to numb out in the same fashion that other soul ages do. It may work for younger souls, but it doesn't take long for the old soul to realize that it's not working, and so those phases are usually short-lived.

Even though something like television or the internet may seem trivial, the more you grow as a soul, the more you'll see each and every thought and action as something that can either be used to further your spiritual growth or create a diversion from that process. And either way is just fine, as long as you're not in denial that there is an effect. Remember, every thought, action and belief is either medicine or poison; there is no neutral.

Old souls are willing to see themselves clearly and take responsibility, sometimes to a fault. The concept of inappropriate responsibility and guilt comes up often in the old soul. When someone acts unkindly to an old soul, they'll typically think that there's something wrong with themselves, rather than thinking that the other person is just having a bad day or has their own issues.

We've got self-blame on one hand and feeling victimized on the other. The victimization is a hold-over from time spent in the fourth level of soul development, and the consistent self-blame signifies the entry into the old soul realm. This leads us to the biggest thought challenge for old souls: the illusion of powerlessness. It's present in most old souls, until they move through it and discover their personal power. That discovery can lead to a release of old relationships, jobs, and even family connections. When you realize that you have the right to feel good, after many years of training people to expect martyr-like behavior from you, it makes sense that the adjustment can be too much for some people and you may experience some backlash.

Eventually, any guilt that you feel for protecting yourself from other people's emotional violence or other types of violence will fade away and you'll feel wonderful for correcting the issue that created that scenario in the first place. That issue is always some version of self-betrayal. It may be that your mind and your body wanted to keep the peace, to such an extreme that you betrayed what your soul knew was right for you. Or that you so desperately wanted your spouse or partner or family member to avoid feeling pain or rejection or abandonment that you caused yourself pain, rejected yourself and abandoned yourself on a soul level.

Most old souls will go through a period of entanglement, codependency and over-empathy, until they've given themselves permission to actually love and support themselves in the deep, pure way that's natural to the soul.

Remember that *the soul's natural state is freedom*. For that liberation to be re-discovered, we must uncover our personal power and take action on our own behalf.

Empathy

em·pa·thy

ˈempəTHē/

noun
1. the ability to understand and share the feelings of another.

Upgrading Empathy through Enlightenment

The empathy myth tells us that when we feel empathy, it hurts or it's painful. Typically, when we empathize (and those of us who are old souls do that almost constantly), we're used to our empathy causing us pain. If we hear a terrible news story, or a friend is suffering with a deep loss, those of us who have high levels of empathy will tend to feel the feelings of the other people involved, very deeply. I heard a story from a client recently, where she recounted a crime that had been committed, in which a 15-year-old girl was drugged and assaulted.

If she would have told me that story several years ago, I would've deeply empathized with everyone involved and felt sick, sad and overwhelmed. I would've held onto those feelings for the rest of the day, and maybe into the next few days. And I would've identified with the 15-year-old girl and felt the sense of victimization, pain, fear, etc. My language would've supported that, too, such as, "She must've been so terrified. Oh, my goodness, she must be in so much shock and pain! What can I do to help?"

Fast forward to more recent years, I've healed the majority of issues within myself that resonate with:

1. being 15 years old in this lifetime (solar plexus chakra)
2. my lifetimes as an adolescent soul (solar plexus chakra)
3. being assaulted (root chakra)
4. my lifetimes as an infant soul (root chakra)
5. shock, pain and terror (heart and upper chakras)

This healing led to my reaction being different. My upgraded empathy reaction was to deeply identify and understand the feelings of the 15-year-old girl, to understand the feelings of the parents, and to understand the feelings of the perpetrator... but the pain only came when I got to the parents. When I thought of them, my heart started hurting and all of the "normal" feelings of empathy came to the surface. Because I had healed all of the issues that would get triggered by the girl's suffering, I wasn't carrying that pain around. But when it came to the parents, I still have some healing to do from that perspective, so the pain was with me for a bit. This tells me that I still have some healing to do around my being a parent, not having control of my child's experience, and watching my child suffer during the hardships of life.

Painful empathic feelings only stick around when we're unhealed in that area. This is nothing like being numb or uncaring; it's about compassion without holding pain. This is upgraded empathy, which occurs on your way to enlightenment.

Whether that wound is from this lifetime or another, it's there, or I wouldn't have experienced empathy in that way—where it hurts and lingers like it's my own pain. So what does this tell us about upgrading empathy through our enlightenment process?

What Is the Accurate Way to Perceive Reality when Someone Is Assaulted?

It can be hard to swallow that an innocent person allowed a terrible thing to happen to them for their own healing and development, and that everyone involved agreed to be part of that process with and for them. This is why some people who have been victimized can have years and years of therapy, and still ask the question, "What did I do to deserve that?" or "Why do I still feel responsible for what happened to me?"

Traditional psychology will tell you, "You didn't do anything to deserve abuse; it was all the perpetrator's fault, there was nothing you could've done to change it, so let go of any sense of responsibility there." And when we're solely identified with the physical world, we feel very sorry that we (or anyone else) went through any suffering. We'll say, "I'm so sorry that you had to go through that." And in the physical world, that is all true.

As I'm not a psychologist, I can only speak to what

I'll call the "soul psychology" of being victimized. On a spiritual level, we all know the highest level truth about the events in our lives. We know (not always consciously, but many times unconsciously) that we have elected to participate in every event, every trauma, every relationship, every situation that happens in this lifetime, for our soul's growth and to help others grow as well. So, while I fully identify with and understand and feel someone else's pain (as well as my own), when painful things happen... am I "sorry" that it happened? No, because I know why it happened and I understand the free will/sovereign component of our souls.

In the spiritual world, before you were born, you knew what you wanted to learn in this lifetime and you learned that there were several ways for you to obtain that healing and development. You chose the ways that you felt would guarantee your forward movement. And if your goal was to fully understand victimization or to heal the root chakra or whatever it was, then you set up the circumstances for it to happen the way it did.

Now, that doesn't mean that if we change our minds, we're stuck in a sort of contract. We are sovereign in our own lives; we can change our minds, invoke our free will, and choose a different path. We can choose to coast through this life and not learn those hard lessons, and slow down our soul's progress. Most of the time though, we stick pretty close to the choices we made in our life between lives.

When we change our minds about one of our lessons before we've reached a pretty high level of spiritual evolution, we tend to experience short-term regret when we get to the other side. This happens many times when someone commits suicide. They will feel regret for a short while, and then they'll move into the next phase of their healing on the other side, which includes amplifying self-love, forgiveness and understanding.

When empathy goes haywire and takes over—where you feel other people's feelings without any control or relief, and you feel overwhelmed on a regular basis by other people's feelings—you know that those are feelings and areas of pain that are ready to be healed within you. When I was with an ex, I had such a hard time leaving when the relationship became verbally abusive because, yes, I loved him, but the higher level truth was that I was afraid that he would feel abandoned. I didn't want to ever "make" someone feel abandoned. So for a while, I was willing to sacrifice my own self-respect, self-honoring and happiness to try to avoid making him feel abandoned.

There were two main things wrong with my theory. One, I had put someone else's wellbeing far above my own. Two, I wasn't identifying my own fear of abandonment and my own abandonment issues. When we heal our own stuff, we don't ever sacrifice or martyr ourselves so someone else can avoid healing their stuff. It just doesn't make sense! You cannot take away someone else's lessons, just like you can't avoid your own. However, you can make yourself miserable by trying to do what you can't do.

Before we were born, my ex and I agreed to come together in this lifetime to help each other heal. I agreed to hold the energy of empathy and teach him what that looks like, and he agreed to teach me boundaries. We have to remember that our job is to hold the energy that we agreed to, and that how it's received isn't our business. I'm not sure if he learned the empathy lesson, but if he didn't learn it from me, there are many other people that he made agreements with who can model that for him. I certainly learned the boundary lesson! Boundaries are an ongoing process for me, but for the most part, I got a Master's level class with him, and every time I think of him, I have no resentment at all, even though he was verbally and psychologically abusive. When I think of him, I say to him in my mind, "Thank you for being my teacher," and I truly mean it.

Before the two of us were born, when those agreements were made between us, he knew that he was going to lose a lot by helping me with my boundaries lesson. He knew that the best, most effective way to teach someone boundaries is by steamrolling them. He also knew that he would lose the relationship with me by doing that. He knew that friends and family would be horrified by the way he was treating me. He knew that even his work would be compromised by his behavior. And still, he agreed to bring that lesson to me, full force, and I'm appreciative. I was a good student, and I truly got it.

I knew that showing him empathy as a way of life was going to be painful for me. I knew that I was going to endure some abuse to share the empathy with him. I knew that no one had held the energy of empathy steady for him, and that I was so ingrained with empathic traits, I was a great candidate to show him that. And I did a good job. Whether or not he received it is not my business. How you choose to view the events is what leads to your peace.

If you choose to see everything in your life as a positive event, you'll get positive results from everything in your life.

If you're on a spiritual path of some sort, and you decide that you're tired of things being really hard, or tired of always learning through deep loss or pain, you can choose to get the lessons that you agreed to, in a different, upgraded way. It just requires a declaration. This doesn't mean that you'll never experience hard things or pain again; it means that you'll have more access to the wisdom that you've gathered from all of your incarnations and your time on the other side, and you'll use that wisdom to make your road less tumultuous. When challenging things happen, you'll perceive them more accurately, and thus have less pain.

Activating the Universal Law of Declaration

In a quiet, relaxed moment, repeat the following Declaration three times.

"In the highest and purest light under grace, I give thanks for and I retain all of the wisdom that I've gained through painful learning experiences in this life. I now declare, as a sovereign being of light, that I am open, willing and ready to learn through experiences of love, fulfillment, happiness and joy. So be it.

~ ~ ~

Livelihood

Another one of the biggest differences between younger souls and old souls is career. Younger souls can be perfectly happy and content working in a corporate environment or the same job for a long time. Stability is important, and being part of team tends to work for them. But as their soul develops, many folks start to feel like the typical 9 to 5 just isn't working anymore.

There are passions that begin to wake up within you as your soul naturally grows. Sometimes several areas of interest will start to call to you, in need of your heart's attention. When you make that shift from the head (work that doesn't inspire you) to the heart (whatever really lights you up), dissatisfaction with the "head"-based work can start to bubble up.

When your soul is growing, part of what's happening is movement from body- or mind-based living into soul- and spirit-based living. Here's an example that just happened in my own life:

I live in the soul/spirit energy most of the time. I came home from work recently, after channeling intense healing with clients all day, completely filled with so much soul and spirit energy. Our excited 70-pound puppy, Bodhi, came bounding over to me and in his exuberance, put his big teeth on my hand and started to chomp down. I felt physical pain and fear and quickly, instinctively, moved from the soul/spirit energy into the mind/body energy. That prompted me to loudly say "No!" and try to swat him on his hindquarter.

Most people would say that was a normal response, that a dog needs correction in that way, and that there's nothing wrong with that reaction. I heard that from my loved ones who witnessed it. But because I live so deeply in the soul/spirit energy, it startled me to move into the mind/body so quickly and I immediately started crying. The emotion was because I had attempted to use force to overpower another living thing, and that's not in alignment with where I typically live (energetically). It was such a contrast.

I share this story with you so that you can know the two main energies that pull us out of the soul and spirit energy (our natural state) and into the mind and body energy (naturally designed to be the support system for the soul and spirit, not the driver).

Those two energies are pain and fear.

It can be physical pain, emotional pain, repressed pain, unaddressed pain, your pain, someone else's pain... it doesn't matter. It can be rational fear, irrational fear, completely understandable fear, totally made-up fear... it doesn't matter. On the surface, you might feel that there isn't much pain or fear in your life today, and if so, that's great! Just know that as you move through your soul's healing and development, there will be feelings that come to your mind or manifest as illness in your body, that maybe you hadn't realized were still living inside you. Sometimes these residues are decades or even lifetimes old.

~ ~ ~

Here are a few questions that might bring some things to light:

- Were you ever bullied when you were a child, even for one day? (fear of not being accepted and the pain of being victimized)

- Did you ever feel unwanted? (fear of not being good enough and the pain of feeling unwanted or unimportant)

- Do you make excuses for your parents, as to why they couldn't give you what you needed? (fear of not being worthy of getting what you need and the pain of parental confusion)

- Do you have any emotional triggers that cause you to act out and feel emotionally out of control? (fear of being victimized and the pain of taking things personally)

- Is your inner voice pretty critical of you? (fear of not being good enough, attractive enough, and/ or smart enough and the pain of self-betrayal)

- Were you ever cheated on, or did you ever cheat on someone? (fear of not getting the love you wanted and the pain of feeling unloved and disconnected)

Why is it important to address these past pains and fears? The process of healing and clearing out these residues are a huge part of the growth of the soul. Do you remember that the soul's natural state is freedom? That freedom and liberation doesn't just pop up one day and you feel completely free and liberated from all pain and fear (although I'm sure it could happen that way if we, as human beings, allowed it).

The way it happens is through us addressing every hurt and fear, and washing it over with so much unconditional love that the memory and the feeling literally change and reveal the true nature of the experience—a challenge that was designed to help you grow and embody more love. This brings us back to the concept of enlightenment, or perceiving reality accurately. When we are truly enlightened to a specific situation or condition, we see it accurately as the challenge that is helping us remember more of our true nature, which is love, love, love! Seeing things clearly is an incredible gift, and an integral part of this process.

Here is the most important concept that must be clear for you at this level: All betrayal is self-betrayal. You might be thinking that I'm crazy, because when your ex cheated on you, *he* betrayed you, right? And when you were fired so the boss's friend could take your job, you were betrayed. And when your parents didn't give you what you needed, that felt like betrayal.

The truth of these examples (and every situation that you could throw at me to test this truth) is this. All betrayal is self-betrayal for one reason: Anytime anyone has ever done anything to hurt you, if you internalized it and allowed the pain and fear to take up residence within you as a response or a reaction to the situation or person, your soul does not understand your position. Your mind and body will fully support the position of "victim" or "betrayed" or "unworthy" or whatever. But your soul and spirit know that this is not the highest truth, and that everything that ever happens in your life—painful or not, fearful or not—is for your highest good, and is an *exercise* for you to grow on a soul level. If the situation isn't being used in that way, if you're resisting that process, then you are in the energy of self-betrayal and your soul won't be soothed until it's released.

The overall growth of the old soul will be focused on the issues of the throat, brow and crown chakras, which include:

- A deep desire to be heard and understood
- A fear of expressing the real truth or a habit of over-expressing
- Over-empathizing with others
- "If I do what I really want to do, then others won't love me."
- "More than anything, I want to trust my intuition."
- A deep knowing that there is more to life than this
- Difficulty making decisions that are best for you
- Questioning organized religion
- Lack of commitment when it comes to joining groups and following through
- A need to be needed
- Working on trusting self, the inner guru
- Learning that it's okay to be happy, even when others aren't

The throat chakra is the bridge between the head

and the heart. When you're feeling like your head and your heart aren't in harmony— that your mind wants one thing while your heart wants another—the problem is that there's something that hasn't been honestly expressed. It could be that you're not being honest with yourself, and haven't expressed your truth within. It could also be that you're too concerned with not disappointing others, that you're not being honest about what you really need and want. The best action to take is to engage the throat chakra by writing, journaling about everything you see, feel and know right now.

As you journal, ask yourself these leading questions:

1. What do I see in this situation? Answer using only your observation; this is the brow chakra in action.

2. What do I feel? Answer from the heart— how you truly feel, not how you want to feel. Your heart knows.

3. What do I know? This is your crown chakra activating. You don't have to have an answer to this question. Just asking the question starts the healing process.

How do you know if it's time to heal the throat, brow and crown chakras?

- If you have trouble trusting your intuition
- If you find yourself in situations that don't feel true to you, but you feel obligated
- If you have a hard time speaking up for yourself

- If you feel like you lack a tactful way of expressing your truth
- If you want to journal or write, but are resisting the urge, or can't make yourself do it
- If you feel overly responsible for other people's issues
- If worry derails you
- If there are times when you feel so overwhelmed with anxiety that it's hard to function
- If you have a tendency toward dizziness or vertigo
- If you have thyroid, neck or throat issues
- If you have regular migraines or sinus issues
- If you have severe trouble with your hearing or eyesight, that's not age-related
- If you have questions about your spirituality, religion or place in the spiritual world

Here are some tools to help you heal and continue your journey into enlightenment.

Affirmations

I am sovereign, I am free.

I can trust myself, all is well.

My connection with the Divine is unbreakable.

(continued on next page)

Clear, loving expression is natural for me.

I lovingly accept myself fully.

I see the Divine in all things, including myself.

Centering

Close your eyes and sense a bright white light coming down from the heavens and entering the top of your head. This light completely fills you on every level, and encompasses you completely. As you count down from 10 to 1, all of your energy centers are ignited by this pure light and brought into perfect alignment with each other. Count down now from 10 to 1. When you're complete, say, "I allow this centering to continue, even while I'm not focused on it."

(Anytime you feel intuitively or spiritually blocked, return to this centering moment.)

Mantra

Om Shanti Om (meaning: I am peace)

or

The Ho'oponopono Mantra:

I'm sorry. Please forgive me. I love you. Thank you.

This mantra, repeated again and again, helps to clear away old patterns that lead us to act and feel out of habit, instead of inspiration. This mantra is one of the simplest, yet most beneficial techniques to move out of the overwhelm that can be associated with being an old soul, and into the peace of a more developed old soul. I can't recommend this enough. It's also a good remedy for insomnia when your mind just won't turn off.

For a free recording of these mantras and other audios that you can listen to and gain the benefits from, even while you sleep, visit our special webpage for readers of this book: alyssamalehorn.com/hoiys

Mudra

Anjali Mudra

Anjali Mudra

Benefits: Activates the corpus callosum, bridging the two hemispheres of the brain. Creates a sense of centeredness and quiet. Calms the energy of overwhelm, especially in intense circumstances.

Technique: Sit in a comfortable position, and with your palms in facing each other in front of your chest in prayer position. Relax your shoulders. Hold for 5 to 45 minutes, incorporating a mantra or an affirmation from this chapter if you like.

Guided Meditation

For a free recording of this meditation and other audios that you can listen to and follow along with, visit our special webpage for readers of this book: alyssamalehorn.com/ hoiys

Take a few deep breaths, and start to let the air flow all the way down into your belly. Relax your stomach and your hips, allowing yourself to fully breathe... slowly and gently. As you read this, say "Thank you" to all of your Divine helpers, guides, angels, and the Great Spirit. You may want to hold your hands in prayer position in front of your heart center as you read.

You're going to invite in the energy that you need for your healing and to support your awakening. Sense the brightest and purest white light, coming down from the heavens and filling your body. This pristine light is swirling all around you, and you can feel its cleansing energy. Allow the light to permeate every cell of your being, using your imagination to envision every part of you becoming saturated with this light.

As you breathe deeply and allow yourself to feel the

relaxing energy of this light, begin to notice that the bright white light is taking on a blue or violet hue. Whatever color comes to your mind is the perfect color energy for you at this moment.

Remember, there is nothing else you need to be doing right now; this moment is the most important moment you have. This blue or violet light now begins to focus within your throat or your head. Wherever you sense that light focusing is exactly right for you, for right now.

You're inviting your Highest Self, that Mighty I AM presence within you, to now descend into your physical body to the degree that it is most benevolent for you at this time. You may feel warm, you may feel relaxed, you may feel even a little sleepy as this occurs. This connection of the Higher Self with the lower self (the physical body) is a natural part of your evolution. This is a process that you've been waiting for, whether you were aware of it or not.

The energy that you've stored from the past (in your throat, brow and crown chakras) is now being assessed by your Highest Self. The wisest, most enlightened aspect of you is now choosing what energies to keep—those energies that you're still working with and learning from. These could be energies of all types, from many lifetimes, from many circumstances.

As you continue to breathe, allow your shoulders to relax and give thanks for the innate wisdom of your Divine Higher Self. You're now allowing what's no longer needed to be dispersed from your energy field and your chakras, and it's being released with every exhale, back to Source.

Now you're going to address the things that you've stored in the throat, brow and crown chakras, the things that you've stored through ancestral patterns, lineage issues, past lifetimes, and this lifetime. You've needed everything that you've stored in these chakras up until this point. Now you'll choose what you need and what you don't more consciously.

Everything you've stored in these chakras has also affected your cells, your organs, your systems. It's affected you physically, mentally, emotionally, and spiritually. Here you are, making conscious choices about what you want to include. So begin by giving thanks for all of the wisdom, love, and everything you've gotten, either from this lifetime, other lifetimes, from your ancestors, or from your lineage.

Give thanks for everything you've learned from the challenging aspects, and from the obvious blessings, from some of the things that weren't so easy and some of the things that flowed beautifully. Give thanks for all of the wonderful things that have been brought to you, such as the energies of intuition, expression and connection. As you give thanks, you're amplifying the positive energies, including the energies of freedom and the knowing that all IS well, no matter what.

Give thanks to all of this in all aspects of time and space, and in all aspects of you—physical, emotional, mental, ethereal, astral—in every possible way, including factors that are known to you, and factors that are unknown.

It's time to give thanks for and to release any and all of the following that are no longer serving you. You are now releasing those energies that you no longer need, either from this lifetime, past lifetimes, ancestral, and lineage issues. This includes any and all lack of acceptance of your physical body, self-judgment, and self-criticism. As you're reading this, you're neutralizing and releasing the energies of overwhelm, insecurity, disconnection, fear, and blocked intuition.

Breathe deeply and allow the fears of connection and disconnection to swirl and gently release from your throat, brow and crown, up into the ether, back to Divine Source. You're neutralizing and giving thanks for all of the lessons and everything that you've learned—all of the wisdom and all of the love. And now, you will complete that releasing of any of these that you are no longer using, and any others that I did not mention that are not in your highest good, that you're no longer working with. As you count down from ten to one you will release what you no longer need, whatever is no longer to your highest benefit, and no longer helping you achieve your highest good and your own joy. As you count down from ten to one, you'll neutralize and release that. Ten, nine, eight, seven, six, five, four, three, two, one. Take a deep breath, and now release it. Perfect.

You may feel calm, centered, lightheaded, relaxed or excited. If you feel emotional, know that is okay; just let it keep flowing through. You're only releasing what your Higher Self has agreed to release, what you are done with. Keep breathing.Imagine that you have deep roots coming from the base of your spine and the bottoms of your feet that go all the way down into the core of the Earth. These deep roots can be like tree roots; they can be like cables. Whatever they are, they're keeping you grounded, and centered, and reminding you of your sense of safety, your sense of security. That is real. You are safe. All is well.

Now you're going to create healing from all of your lifetimes. Affirm: "I allow all appropriate, optimal, beneficial, and benevolent healing from all of my lifetimes, from the moment of birth to the present moment. Now allow your glands that are associated with these chakras to be upgraded. The glands are the thyroid, pituitary, pineal, or the energy of those. If you no longer have these glands, the energy of those glands are still present in your body at this time, and you are updating and upgrading those glands. Right now, all of the frequencies in your body are being harmonized. They're being optimized. Your glands, your organs, your systems, your blood, all the water in your body— they're being upgraded and optimized. Give thanks for the awareness of your own body, and embrace the optimal connection with your own voice, with your knowing and intuition, and your connection to your Higher Self and the Divine.

As you count down from ten to one, you'll allow this healing to complete. Ten, nine, eight, seven, six, five, four, three, two, one. Take a deep breath, and now exhale. Allow whatever comes to your mind, to come. All is well. Now just keep breathing. Be present in your body. There's no rush. You have plenty of time. When you're complete, stretch, take a deep breath and make some notes about what you've experienced.

~ CHAPTER 8 ~

CONCLUSION

AT THIS POINT, YOU'VE LEARNED ABOUT the motivations, struggles, gifts, archetypes and blessings of each soul age. You've probably determined where you currently fit in this ever-evolving structure. At this point, you've experienced some healing of your old wounds and feelings of limitations that were holding you back. You've enhanced your soul's progress through having more understanding of yourself and the people in your life.

There are three main concepts I want to reiterate as we wrap up. Two of them are: 1) The younger the soul, the more it is motivated by fear, and 2) The older the soul, the more motivated it is by love. These are important concepts because the harboring of fear energy keeps us from easily moving forward in our own natural growth process. Fear is resistance to higher-level understanding and higher-level living.

This is not to say that older souls don't have fear! Every one of us, at every stage of soul development, will experience fear on some level. This is part of the human experience. Older souls can even experience terror, and many have found themselves in terrifying life-and-death type situations.

The way I've defined enlightenment is, "perceiving

reality accurately," meaning, without fear. *True reality* is devoid of fear, and is full of love and a sense of peace. How easy it is to become distracted or even obsessed with the energy of fear, as it's all around us, all the time. Making a conscious decision to honor the fear (the illusion), and then to release it in favor of a more innate energy of love is a brave and completely normal thing to do. It's also rebellious, in that you're moving against the inertia of the collective consciousness, the younger souls who are digging their heels into what they feel is the true reality (the fear-based lifestyle). If you haven't thought of peace and love being rebellious acts before, stay tuned! It'll become more and more rebellious, as the frequency of the planet increases and fear keeps skyrocketing among the younger and adolescent soul ages.

What an interesting time we've chosen to incarnate into! There are so many opportunities to practice feeling love, practice releasing fear, and practice being centered. That's one of the reasons that you and I chose to incarnate at this time in history. There is a waiting list of souls that want to incarnate on this planet for that very reason. This place is the most challenging of all of the planetary schools; there's nowhere else to get an education like this. Earth is the Harvard of the cosmic schools, and you're doing it. You chose to be here, and you're doing it! Remember, on a soul level you are always getting what you want. What your soul wants to learn (through contrast and exercises) will always be the motivator of your experience.

You're allowed to be proud of yourself, what you've been through here, and what you've accomplished. It's worth noting that the only accomplishments that we carry forward into the spirit world are the ones where we've chosen love over fear. In every situation, you have a choice. There are great tools to help you release what's no longer serving you, whether in this book, with spiritual and holistic practitioners, or on your own, in meditation or other healing modalities. There is no "one size fits all" method to moving through this life and into these higher levels of awareness.

It's the daily interactions—the small things, the reactions to others, the conscious choice to love, the conscious choice to hold boundaries for yourself—that bring you peace and safety. Moving into these higher levels does not mean that you allow people to walk all over you because you're blissed out and have no boundaries! It means that you, through the energy of self-love and self-respect, create happy boundaries that feel great to you, that allow you the freedom to interact with people in your life, while feeling safe and well.

Remember the mantra, "Lokah samastah sukhino bhavantu." May all living beings be happy and free (and this includes me).

The third concept that must be completely understood to continue on your spiritual path with a clear understanding of what's really happening is that, spiritually, we are truly all in this together. We're all growing through the same natural process—at varying levels and with varying intensity—but make no mistake: there is no spiritual difference in value between you and the person sitting in the car next to you in traffic or the President of the United States or the homeless veteran struggling to survive. You are noticing that person because there is something you're learning from them being in your life, and vice versa. Of course, there are no coincidences.

It's one of my most heartfelt wishes that this book will bring a sense of unity and compassion to people who were otherwise focused on the differences between us. As we elevate our understanding of every soul phase, we can sense the differences and make conscious choices about what's good for us, without judging someone else as good or bad, right or wrong. This book has not been about how different we are when we're in the varying soul phases. Ultimately, it's about the journey that we're all on together. As I mentioned earlier, this planet is like an all-ages one-room schoolhouse that can be considered chaos or fun, but either way, it's an adventure.

This time on Earth is both exciting and challenging for all of us. What a blessing to be here together! I've thoroughly enjoyed being your guide on this journey through the soul ages. It's my honor to help elevate your awareness of yourself, others and your time here. Breathe deeply, and enjoy the ride. Blessings to you.

ABOUT THE AUTHOR

ALYSSA MALEHORN is a spiritual teacher, soul guide, psychic medium and divine transmitter of healing energies for the purpose of illuminating and demystifying the path to enlightenment. Her mission is to empower, educate and enlighten all truth-seekers, in all aspects of life. Alyssa is a catalyst for transformational healing, wisdom, and joy for individuals and groups worldwide. She sees the spiritual meaning hidden within all events, from the everyday to global, and is a leader in the empowerment of those seeking freedom from overwhelm and fear.

Alyssa is the creator of the life-changing, online *Spirit Within: Spiritual Awakening Program*, and the divinely inspired, best-selling programs *Discover Your Divine Team: Spirit Guides, Archangels & Ascended Masters; Awakening & Ascension: Building Your Light Quotient; Channeled Light Healing; In The Light: State Of The Universe,* and more.

Information about individual and couple's consultations, speaking engagements, group workshops, meditation events, Reiki and healing classes (in Austin, Texas, as well as Sedona, Arizona, Southern California and other areas) is available at alyssamalehorn.com.

Alyssa lives in Austin, Texas with her spiritual partner, Zack, happy dog, Bodhi, and talkative cat, Daisy.

CPSIA information can be obtained
at www.ICGtesting.com
Printed in the USA
LVOW08s0827160917
548596LV00001B/18/P